The Amazing Almanac

Gyles Brandreth

PELHAM BOOKS

First published in Great Britain by
Pelham Books Ltd
44 Bedford Square
London WC1B 3DU
1981

ISBN 0 7207 1384 6

Printed and bound in Great Britain by
Hollen Street Press Limited, Slough

Introduction

With this book in one hand — and with or without a pint of Carling Black Label in the other — you are certain to learn something new every day of the year. The volume you are now holding is quite simply the world's most unusual almanac of fantastic fascinating facts — amazing pieces of information that may sound incredible but are actually absolutely true.

I have been collecting amazing information ever since I discovered that Jayne Mansfield and Marie Antoinette shared identical bust measurements. On the next day I happened to find out that Queen Zingua of Angola was in the habit of beheading her many lovers the morning after the night before. A week later I learnt that William III, Queen Anne, George I, George II, George III and George VI all died on Sundays — and then there was no stopping me. Admittedly nothing you will find in the pages that follow is as *useful* as anything you learnt at school, but I hope you will agree with me that most of it is a lot more entertaining!

If I weren't naturally somewhat shy as a person I might feature in the book myself — on 10 February 1977 I tossed the world's tiniest pancake; on 13 February 1978 I spoke non-stop for eleven hours; on 23 November 1979 I became the first person to stand on his head in the House of Lords — and perhaps in the next edition I will. Perhaps you will too because if you have a piece of amazing information that is provable and relates to a particular day of the year, let me know all about it and I will hope to include it in the next edition. And if what you tell me is amazing enough you will be amply rewarded because the individual who submits what I judge to be the most amazing piece of information will receive a year's supply of Carling Black Label — that's 365 cans, provided you are over eighteen. If you have an amazing fact — or several of them — fill in the form at the back of the book and send it to me by 30 June 1982.

Cheers!

January

HAPPY NEW YEAR!

January 1st marks the birthday of Idi Amin, Jacky Ickx and Paul Revere. It is also the day on which the Commonwealth of Australia was formed in 1901.

In 1975 Australian chickens were used to control traffic in a park in Melbourne.

THE *DAILY UNIVERSAL REGISTER* CHANGED ITS NAME ON 1 JANUARY 1788. IT BECAME THE WORLD'S MOST FAMOUS NEWSPAPER, *THE TIMES.*

The Union of Soviet Socialist Republics was proclaimed on 1 January 1923. If the U.S.S.R. were the size of a football pitch, the world's smallest country, the Vatican City, would be no bigger than one quarter of a postage stamp.

THE NATIONALIST GOVERNMENT IN CHINA WAS ESTABLISHED ON 1 JANUARY 1926. CHINA HAS THE WORLD'S LARGEST POPULATION. IT HAS NEARLY TWICE AS MANY INHABITANTS AS INDIA, THE WORLD'S SECOND LARGEST POPULATION, AND ALMOST ONE PERSON IN FOUR LIVING ON EARTH IS CHINESE.

Lawn Tennis has developed from a game originally played by French monks in monastery cloisters during the eleventh century.

January

2
King Zog of Albania was deposed from his throne on 2 January 1946. Albania once issued a postage stamp in celebration of the country's leading chain-smoker, Ahmed Zog I, who smoked 240 cigarettes a day.

2 January is Berchtold's Day in Switzerland. The Swiss are famous for their chocolate – and for their chocolate consumption. Enough chocolate is sold in Switzerland to provide every citizen with two big bars every day.

THE FIRST ROCKET TO FLY NEAR THE MOON, LUNA I, WAS LAUNCHED ON 2 JANUARY 1959. THE MOON'S EQUATORIAL DIAMETER IS ONLY ONE QUARTER THAT OF THE EARTH'S.

The first set of traffic lights ever erected blew up outside the Houses of Parliament on 2 January 1869, killing the policeman operating them.

3
The Roman orator and politician, Marcus Tullius Cicero, was born on 3 January 106 BC. The total population of the world during his lifetime was only equal to the number by which the current world population *increases* in just two years.

Alaska achieved its statehood as the 49th state of the U.S.A. on 3 January 1954. The state covers such a large area that were it an independent country, it would rank after Mongolia as the eighteenth largest country on earth.

HENRY V'S QUEEN, CATHERINE DE VALOIS, DIED ON 3 JANUARY 1437, AND WAS BURIED IN WESTMINSTER ABBEY. DURING REBUILDING WORK IN THE REIGN OF HENRY VIII, HER MUMIFIED BODY WAS DUG UP AND LEFT IN AN OPEN BOX, WHERE IT REMAINED ON SHOW FOR TWO HUNDRED YEARS, BEFORE BEING BURIED ONCE AGAIN IN 1776.

January

4 King Charles I attempted to arrest five members of Parliament on 4 January 1642, an act that led to the outbreak of the Civil War.

The author of the classic French novel La Peste (The Plague), *Albert Camus, died on 4 January 1960. During the fourteenth century, an estimated total of 75,000,000 people died from the plague, including one in four of the population of Europe.*

DOORMICE WERE ONCE CONSIDERED A POPULAR DELICACY AMONGST THE INHABITANTS OF ANCIENT ROME.

Louis Braille, the inventor of the Braille reading system for the blind, was born on 4 January 1809. His invention was a particular favourite with another great inventor, Thomas Edison, who preferred to read Braille, although he could read perfectly well with his eyes.

5 The inventor of the Gillette safety-razor, King Gillette, was born on 5 January 1855. After inventing his revolutionary razor he was disappointed that he did not sell more than 51 razors and 168 blades during his first year in business. However, in the following year sales soared to a total of 90,000 razors and nearly 12,500,000 blades.

The famous long-distance pilot, Amy Johnson, died in an air crash on 5 January 1941. She was the first woman ever to fly solo from England to Australia. A scarf knitted from all the wool produced in Australia in one year would stretch for two hundred times the distance of Amy's epic flight.

THE MOST POPULAR SPORT PLAYED IN AMERICAN NUDIST CAMPS IS VOLLEYBALL.

Catherine de Medici died on 5 January 1589. During her life she had been wife to one King of France and mother to three others. 7

January

6

The former American president, Theodore Roosevelt, died on 6 January 1919. He left behind one immortal souvenir — the teddy bear, which was named after him.

King Richard II was born on 6 January 1367. Extravagant with clothes and jewels, his only lasting claim to fame is that he probably invented the handkerchief.

6 JANUARY, WHICH NOWADAYS IS TWELFTH NIGHT, USED TO BE CHRISTMAS DAY ON THE OLD CALENDAR.

Jet propulsion was invented on 6 January 1944. The world's fastest jet aircraft has flown at a speed of just under 2,200 mph.

IN SPITE OF THEIR FEARSOME APPEARANCE, GORILLAS NEVER KILL FOR FOOD, THEY ARE STRICT VEGE-TARIANS.

You can clean your teeth as effectively by brushing them with salt as you can by using toothpaste.

7

On 7 January 1785, the first balloon crossing of the English Channel took place. The success of this flight cost the two aviators a suit of clothes each, and their dignity. In a desperate final effort to each the safety of the French coast, they had to ditch all that they were wearing, and so arrived safe, but naked, in France.

Pope Innocent X died on 7 January 1655. The ancient custom of kissing the Pope's toe lasted for over one thousand years, before being abolished in 1773.

JOSEPH BONAPARTE, THE KING OF NAPLES, WAS BORN ON 7 JANUARY 1768. IN THE SEVENTY-FIVE YEARS BETWEEN 1783 AND 1857, OVER 111,000 NEAPOLITANS DIED AS A RESULT OF EARTHQUAKES.

January

8 Chequers, in Buckinghamshire, became the official residence of the Prime Minister when Lloyd George moved there on 8 January 1921. The original golliwog was presented to the Prime Minister shortly afterwards and now lives in retirement in the house.

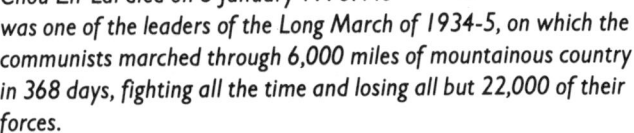

The Chinese military and political leader Chou En-Lai died on 8 January 1976. He was one of the leaders of the Long March of 1934-5, on which the communists marched through 6,000 miles of mountainous country in 368 days, fighting all the time and losing all but 22,000 of their forces.

THE LAST BATTLE EVER FOUGHT BETWEEN ENGLISH AND AMERICAN FORCES TOOK PLACE AT NEW ORLEANS ON 8 JANUARY 1815. THE ENGLISH LOST THE BATTLE WITH 290 DEAD TO THE AMERICANS' TOTAL OF 13. HOWEVER, UNKNOWN TO BOTH ARMIES, THE TWO GOVERNMENTS HAD SIGNED A PEACE TREATY A FORTNIGHT BEFORE THE BATTLE TOOK PLACE.

9 On 9 January 1788, Connecticut became the fifth state to join the U.S.A. An eighteenth century Connecticut law made it illegal to bowl at nine pins, so a tenth pin was added and bowlers have been bowling at ten pins ever since.

The peace treaty between Turkey and Russia was signed at Jassy on 9 January 1792. Between 1812 and 1913 Turkey lost 3 wars to Russia, as well as 2 wars to Egypt and 2 to Greece, not to mention separate defeats in wars against Serbia, Albania and Bulgaria.

THE TRAVELLER, MARCO POLO, WHO SERVED FOR MANY YEARS AT THE COURT OF THE CHINESE EMPEROR, DIED ON 9 JANUARY 1324. THE TRADITIONAL CHINESE SCRIPT HAS OVER 40,000 CHARACTERS.

January

The tomb of the famous Egyptian queen, Cleopatra, was discovered on 10 January 1890. Cleopatra was not only married to her own brother, but she was also mistress to the world's two most powerful men at that time, Julius Caesar and Mark Antony.

The penny post was started in England on 10 January 1840. At the end of the seventeenth century the mail travelled through England at an average speed of 5 mph.

THE FIRST UNDERGROUND RAILWAY LINE IN LONDON WAS OPENED ON 10 JANUARY 1863. TODAY THE LONDON UNDERGROUND STRETCHES FOR 260 MILES BENEATH THE CITY.

The first assembly of the United Nations was held in London on 10 January 1946. The first independent state to be created by the U.N. was Libya.

ELIZABETHAN BROTHELS USED TO SERVE PRUNES, FOR FREE, AT LUNCHTIME.

11

The famous American department-store tycoon, Harry Gordon Selfridge, was born on 11 January 1864. When his famous shop opened in London, he took no less than 97 full-page advertisements in the daily papers in the preceeding six days, and on the opening day sixty policemen had to control the crowds waiting to get inside the new shop.

The famous jockey Fred Archer was born on 11 January 1857. He was champion jockey of England for thirteen years in a row, and during his career rode a total of 2,748 winners. His record run of 246 winners in 1885 remained unbeaten until 1933.

IN ONE YEAR A PRIDE OF 22 LIONS KILLED 1,500 PEOPLE IN KENYA.

January

12 Gunmen tried to murder Al Capone outside a Chicago restaurant on 12 January 1925. Capone escaped unhurt and went on to make a fortune in underworld activities. In 1927 alone he made the equivalent of £21,500,000.

On 12 January 1964, Zanzibar was proclaimed a republic. Earlier in its history the country had fought against Great Britain in a war that lasted thirty-eight minutes.

THE FAMOUS EIGHTEENTH CENTURY POLITICIAN AND ORATOR, EDMUND BURKE, WAS BORN ON 12 JANUARY 1729. MANY OF HIS BEST SPEECHES WERE WRITTEN AFTER HE HAD DRUNK HIMSELF INTO A STUPOR WITH PORT.

A duck is six times less efficient in converting energy into work than a ship.

IT'S POSSIBLE FOR A FEMALE MOSQUITO TO PRODUCE 150,000,000 OFFSPRING IN A YEAR.

13 Today is Canute's Day in Sweden. By an English law written during the reign of King Canute, a woman found guilty of adultery forfeited 'both nose and ears'.

Conscription was introduced in Russia on 13 January 1874. Today the U.S.S.R. has about 3,660,000 troops serving in its armed forces. That is a third as many again as the number serving in U.S. armed forces.

MANY ANCIENT GREEK SOLDIERS USED TO GO INTO BATTLE NAKED FROM THE WAIST DOWN.

The famous Roman consul and general,Gaius Marius died on 13 Jqnuary 86 BC. In one of his most notable victories near Aix en Provence, his forces killed 100,000 Teuton invaders in a fearful two-day battle.

January

14 The author of *Alice in Wonderland*, Lewis Carroll, died on 14 January 1898. He was one of the first child photographers and a mathematician.

The astronomer who gave his name to the famous comet, Edmond Halley, died on 14 January 1742. In 1910 the comet passed within 14,000,000 miles of the earth, which was very close. Apparently the earth passed through the comet's tail.

THE BEE IS THE ONLY INSECT THAT PRODUCES A FOOD EATEN BY MAN.

15 The British Museum was opened on 15 January 1759. During the Second World War the museum was hit by two flying bombs. The second bomb passed exactly through the hole made by the first one and miraculously both bombs failed to explode.

Today is Adult's Day in Japan. The Japanese are the world's second greatest letter writers. In one year alone they write over 13,000,000,000 letters.

POTATO CRISPS WERE INVENTED BY A NORTH AMERICAN INDIAN CHIEF NAMED GEORGE CRUM.

The Irish Free State came into being on 15 January 1922. There are no snakes in Ireland. Tradition holds that they were all banished by St. Patrick.

IN THE U.S.A. YOU CAN DEDUCT ANY MONEY PAID TO A KIDNAPPER AS A RANSOM FROM YOUR INCOME TAX ASSESSMENT.

Tests have shown that cats cannot taste sweet foods.

January

16

Prohibition began in the U.S.A. on 16 January 1920. Fortunately things have changed since then, and the Americans rank amongst the world's leading drinkers. The current record for downing a litre of beer is held by an American. He drained the glass in 1.3 seconds!

On 16 January 1909 the expedition led by Sir Ernest Shackleton reached the magnetic South Pole. Eighty per cent of all the ice on earth is in Antarctica.

SNEEZING USED TO BE CONSIDERED A FAVOURABLE OMEN IN THE ANCIENT WORLD.

When the Mayflower made her famous journey to America she carried the Pilgrim Fathers. On her second voyage she carried a cargo of slaves.

17

One of the leading lights of the American revolution, Benjamin Franklin, was born on 17 January 1706. During his lifetime he was ambassador to France; he helped found the University of Pennsylvania; he invented the rocking chair, bifocals, lightning conductors and a water-powered harmonica and he set up the first postal service in the U.S.A.

Today is St. Anthony's Day. Anthony Trollope, the nineteenth century novelist and author of the Barchester series, was also responsible for introducing letter-boxes into this country.

CLOCKS LOSE WEIGHT AS THEY UNWIND.

The Papal See returned to Rome from Avignon on 17 January 1377. Seventy-nine years later, Pope Calixtos III, issued a papal bull against an apparition in the sky that was terrorizing the Christian world. This was Halley's comet.

THE WATER PRESSURE CONTAINED INSIDE EVERY CELL IN AN ONION WOULD BE ENOUGH TO EXPLODE A STEAM ENGINE.

January

18 On 18 January 1778, Captain Cook discovered Hawaii. The Hawaiian islands are in fact the summits of the tallest mountain range on earth. One mountain on Hawaii, Mauna Kea, measures over 33,000 ft from its submarine base to its summit. This makes it the tallest mountain on earth 4,000 feet higher than Everest.

Peter Mark Roget, the compiler of Roget's Thesaurus was born on 18 January 1779. One word not in his Thesaurus is the longest word in the Oxford English Dictionary, floccipaucinihilpilification, which means 'the action of estimating as worthless'.

TODAY IS A PUBLIC HOLIDAY IN EGYPT, IRAQ, LIBYA AND NIGERIA. IN IRAQ IT'S AGAINST THE LAW TO EAT SNAKES ON A SUNDAY.

Captain Scott's famous expedition reached the South Pole on 18 January 1912. Eight of the world's top ten glaciers are in Antarctica.

19 The great American Civil War general, Robert E. Lee, was born on 19 January 1807. Before accepting the command of the Confederate forces, Lee had turned down the leadership of the Union army.

James Watt, the inventor of the steam engine, was born on 19 January 1736. But the principle of using steam power had been thought of before. Indeed, the modern garden sprinkler is the result of one system of using steam power that was outlined in theory back in ancient Greece.

THE SWORD-BILL HUMMINGBIRD'S BILL IS LONGER THAN ITS BODY.

On 19 January 1966, Mrs Indira Gandhi became Prime Minister of India. More languages are spoken in India than in any other country. Altogether there are 845 languages spoken there.

January

20 Hong Kong was ceded to Britain by China on 20 January 1841. The one cent Hong Kong bank note is the lowest denomination bank note issued. It takes twelve of these to make the equivalent of one English penny.

The English art critic, John Ruskin, died on 20 January 1900. He made a savage attack on the works of the American painter James Whistler, that were exhibited at an exhibition in London in 1877. Whistler took Ruskin to court and the critic lost the case. He was ordered to pay Whistler a farthing in damages.

MAN IS THE ONLY ANIMAL THAT CRIES.

On 20 January 1840, Captain Wilkes discovered the coast of Antarctica. Antarctica is the only continent that is not wider in the north than it is in the south.

EACH OF US PRODUCES 2-3 PINTS OF SALIVA IN OUR MOUTHS EVERY DAY.

Human lungs can hold between five and eight pints of air.

◗◗

21 The great Russian revolutionary leader, V.I. Lenin, died on 21 January 1924. When doctors examined his brain during the post-mortem, they found that it had shrunk to a quarter of its normal size.

Jack Nicklaus was born on 21 January 1940. He is the only golfer ever to win five major championships twice. His total of championship wins (to 1980) is 19, and he has won the U.S. Open four times and been runner-up on seven other occasions.

IT IS THE LARVAE OF MOTHS THAT EAT CLOTHES. THE MOTHS THEMSELVES DO NOT DO THE DAMAGE.

The first nuclear-powered submarine, the U.S. Nautilus, was launched on 21 January 1954. The present-day nuclear-powered submarines are capable of speeds in excess of 35 mph.

January

22

Queen Victoria died on 22 January 1901. Her first action as queen had been to have her bed removed from her mother's bedroom.

The man who some believe wrote the works of Shakespeare, Francis Bacon, was born on 22 January 1561. He died as the result of a severe cold, caught from trying to stuff a chicken with snow, in an experiment on freezing food.

LORD BYRON WAS BORN ON 22 JANUARY 1788. AS A STUDENT AT CAMBRIDGE HE HAD COMPLIED WITH HIS COLLEGE'S RULE OF NOT KEEPING A PET DOG. HE KEPT A BEAR INSTEAD.

23

The principality of Liechtenstein was established in 1719, on 23 January. Today Liechtenstein is a world leader in the export of false teeth.

23 January is a public holiday in Iran. Cyrus the Great, a former ruler of Iran, reportedly knew the name of every man serving in his army.

MOLES CAN DIG TUNNELS ONE HUNDRED YARDS LONG IN A SINGLE NIGHT.

William Pitt died on 23 January 1806. As a young man he became Prime Minister of Great Britain when he was only 24 years old, the youngest man or woman ever to be offered the post.

January

24 Sir Winston Churchill died on 24 January 1965. His father Lord Randolph had died on exactly the same day seventy years before.

Frederick the Great, King of Prussia, was born on 24 January 1712. His father established a famous private guard which consisted of men that averaged well over six feet six inches in height. He made a great effort to recruit tall men into this force, and even went to the lengths of making his guards marry tall women to produce future guardsmen.

THE FIRST DISCOVERY OF GOLD WAS MADE IN CALIFORNIA ON 24 JANUARY 1848, STARTING THE CALIFORNIAN GOLD RUSH. IT TOOK ALMOST HALF A YEAR FOR THE NEWS OF THE STRIKE TO REACH THE EAST COAST OF THE U.S.A.

White is the colour of mourning in China.

PEANUTS ARE USED IN THE MANUFACTURE OF DYNAMITE.

Ice hockey pucks can move over the ice at speeds of over 110 mph.

25 The Scottish poet Robert Burns was born on 25 January 1759. Burns described the haggis as the 'chieftain of the pudding race' and the largest haggis ever made proved him right. It weighed a quarter of a ton and took twelve hours to cook.

Vincent Massey was appointed Governor-General of Canada, the first Canadian-born statesman to achieve the office, on 25 January 1952. Canada has more coastline than any other country. It has a coastline six times longer than that of the smallest continent, Australia.

THE HORN OF A RHINOCEROS IS ACTUALLY HAIR, NOT BONE.

January

26 The largest diamond ever discovered was picked up in a mine in South Africa on 26 January 1905. It weighed $1\frac{1}{4}$ lbs, and while the real stone was sent through the post, a dummy was taken to England under guard.

Today is Australia Day. The town of Mount Isa in Queensland covers an area larger than any other town in the world. It has a total area of 15,822 square miles, which makes it only slightly smaller than the whole of Switzerland.

QUEENSLAND ALSO HAS THE WORLD'S LONGEST FENCE WHICH IS SIX FEET HIGH AND RUNS FOR A DISTANCE OF ALMOST 3,450 MILES.

General Gordon was killed when the Mahdi's troops entered Khartoum on 26 January 1885. The transportation arrangements to the battle of Khartoum, which put down the rebellion, were undertaken by the travel firm of Thomas Cook Ltd.

THE SILK THAT SPIDERS USE TO WEAVE THEIR WEBS IS STRONGER THAN STEEL THREAD OF THE SAME THICKNESS.

27 John Logie Baird gave his first demonstration of television, in public, on 27 January 1926. Today the average American child has watched a total of 710 days of television by the age of eighteen.

The great master of Italian opera, Giuseppe Verdi died on 27 January 1901. One of his most popular works Aida had been commissioned by the khedive of Egypt to celebrate the opening of the Suez Canal.

WOLFGANG AMADEUS MOZART WAS BORN ON 27 JANUARY 1756. FIVE YEARS LATER, HE WAS COMPOSING, AND PLAYING THE PIANO.

Charles Dodgson (Lewis Carroll) was born on 27 January 1832. During his last thirty-seven years he wrote nearly 99,000 letters.

January

28 Peter the Great of Russia died on 28 January 1725. During his life he had his mistress's former lover executed and had the man's head preserved in alcohol and kept by his bed to serve as a warning.

The great Elizabethan navigator, Sir Francis Drake, died on 28 January 1595. When he returned from his first voyage, his ship was packed with booty worth £600,000. Those who had invested in the enterprise were rewarded with a return on their capital that amounted to 4,700 per cent.

THERE WERE SOME DINOSAURS THAT WERE NO LARGER THAN HENS.

Henry VII of England was born on 28 January 1457 and his son Henry VIII died on the same date ninety years later.

BANANA OIL DOES NOT COME FROM BANANAS. IT COMES FROM COAL.

In Venice the junction between two canals is controlled by a set of traffic lights.

29 W.C. Fields was born on 29 January 1879. During the Second World War he even kept £25,000 in Nazi Germany, just in case Hitler won the war.

On 29 January 1820, George III died. During his lifetime he had bought more than 67,000 books, which included 200 bibles, a first edition of Milton's Paradise Lost *and no fewer than 26 books printed by Caxton.*

HUNGARY EXPORTS MORE HIPPOPOTAMUSES THAN ANY OTHER EUROPEAN COUNTRY.

The Victoria Cross was instituted on 29 January 1856. Eleven V.C.s were awarded during the defence of Rorke's Drift, 22-23 January 1879.

January

〜〜〜〜〜〜〜〜〜〜〜〜〜〜〜〜〜〜〜〜〜〜〜〜〜

30

King Charles I was executed on 30 January 1649. Even with his head on the king was only 4 feet 7 inches tall.

The former U.S. president, Franklin D. Roosevelt, was born on 30 January 1882. He was related to five other U.S. presidents by blood and to six others by marriage.

BONE-SETTING USED TO BE UNDERTAKEN BY BLACKSMITHS BEFORE MODERN MEDICINE GAVE THE JOB TO DOCTORS.

On 30 January 1840, the Emperor of China prohibited all trade with Britain. Today China is the world's largest producer of tobacco and camel hair.

BLOND BEARDS GROW FASTER THAN DARK-HAIRED BEARDS.

〜〜〜〜〜〜〜〜〜〜〜〜〜〜〜〜〜〜〜〜〜〜〜〜〜

31

The giant of Victorian seacraft, *The Great Eastern*, was launched on 31 January 1858. The *Queen Elizabeth II*, the largest passenger ship afloat today, has 320 more bedrooms than Buckingham Palace has rooms.

The remote Pacific island of Nauru became independent on 31 January 1968. Nauru has one of the highest standards of living in the world, thanks to its huge deposits of phosphates; created largely out of bird droppings that have been building up for centuries.

THE MOST WIDELY USED DRUG ON EARTH IS THE TRANQUILISER VALIUM.

Queen Beatrix of the Netherlands was born on 31 January 1938. Rotterdam and Amsterdam, the two largest cities in her realm are both below sea-level.

VENUS IS THE ONLY PLANET THAT ROTATES CLOCKWISE.

February

1 Clark Gable was born on 1 February 1907. This star of film hits like *Gone with the Wind* once caused a major slump in the U.S. textile industry. After he appeared naked beneath his shirt in the 1934 film, *It Happened One Night,* overnight men stopped buying vests and several underwear firms went into liquidation.

The Oxford English Dictionary was published for the first time on 1 February 1884. After twenty-two years' work compiling and sorting quotations, the editors had amassed 1$\frac{3}{4}$ tons of paper, that had been submitted by over 800 readers. By publication, one reader alone had sent in 100,000 slips of quotations.

THE BELL ROCK LIGHTHOUSE STARTED OPERATING ON 1 FEBRUARY 1811. THE BRIGHTEST LIGHTHOUSE IN OPERATION IN GREAT BRITAIN TODAY IS THE ONE AT ORFORDNESS IN SUFFOLK. THE BEAM FROM THIS LIGHT IS AS BRIGHT AS 7,500,000 CANDLES.

The United States Supreme Court held its first meeting on 1 February 1790. A century later it ruled that federal income tax violated the Constitution. It wasn't until 1913 that Congress passed the Sixteenth Amendment that made it legal.

DURING THE FIRST WORLD WAR PRESIDENT WILSON'S WIFE TOOK NATIONAL ECONOMY EFFORTS HOME TO THE WHITE HOUSE AND GRAZED A FLOCK OF SHEEP ON THE FAMED FRONT LAWN.

February

2

Today is the feast of the purification of the Virgin Mary. Another virgin who was pure in more than name was Queen Elizabeth I. She was one of the first people in England to install a lavatory in her home (Richmond Palace). And her courtiers were amazed by her fastidiousness. She took a bath at least once a month.

The first public lavatory opened in London on 2 February though this time in 1852. The experiment wasn't a great success though. Only eighty-two members of the public made use of the service in its first month.

THE ROLLS ROYCE 'SILVER SHADOW' USED TO BE CLASSIFIED AS A 'COMPACT CAR' IN AMERICA.

The core of many golf balls consists of castor oil.

3

Greece was created a kingdom on 3 February 1830. King Alexander of Greece died ninety years later after being bitten by his pet monkey, which gave him blood poisoning.

The first English woman doctor was born on 3 February 1821. Her name was Elizabeth Blackwell. If she followed the course of most medical students, she probably increased her vocabulary by 10,000 words during her medical studies.

BLAISE PASCAL, THE BRILLIANT FRENCH MATHEMATICIAN, NAMED AFTER ST. BLAISE, WHOSE DAY THIS IS, INVENTED A CALCULATING MACHINE WHEN HE WAS ONLY 19.

The Russian spacecraft Luna 9 made the first soft landing on the moon on 3 February 1966. Lunar eclipses only occur during a full moon and there can never be more than three lunar eclipses in a year.

February

4

The first man to fly solo across the Atlantic, Charles Lindbergh, was born on 4 February 1902. When he made his epic flight in the *Spirit of St. Louis,* he had to carry such large fuel tanks that he needed a periscope to see where he was flying all the way across the ocean.

A devastating earthquake killed over 23,000 people in Guatemala on 4 February 1976. However, over thirty-six times as many people were killed in the earthquake that hit China in February 1556.

BRICK SOAKED IN PARAFFIN IS ONE OF THE MOST EFFECTIVE BAITS FOR CATCHING LOBSTERS.

The battle of Kumasi ended the Ashanti war in Africa. This campaign was the last time in which British troops went into battle wearing scarlet uniforms.

5

Today is the feast of St. Agatha, the patron saint of bell-founders, by virtue of the similarity of the shape of bells to that of the saint's breasts. The largest bell ever cast weighs 193 tons, stands over 19 feet high, and is 2 feet thick at its thickest point. However, it has never been rung, as it cracked in the foundry, and it's been sitting outside the Kremlin in Moscow ever since.

Today is also a public holiday in Hong Kong, the destination of the first aircraft ever to be hijacked, when in 1948 a band of Chinese bandits took over a flying boat travelling between Macao and Hong Kong.

LEMONS CONTAIN MORE SUGAR THAN STRAWBERRIES.

The Prince of Wales, later King George IV, was declared Prince Regent on 5 February 1811. Fifteen years earlier he had amassed debts which would equal over £12,000,000 today.

February

6

Two British kings died on 6 February. In 1685 Charles II, affectionately nicknamed Old Rowley, after a favourite racehorse, died and 267 years later King George VI died. As Duke of York he had become the only member of the royal family ever to play in the Wimbledon Tennis Championships.

By coincidence, two British queens came into being on the same date. Queen Anne was born on 6 February 1665 and our present Queen Elizabeth II, succeeded to the throne on the death of her father. She is the great grand-daughter thirty-six times removed of King Alfred the Great.

WHEN IT IS CONSIDERED PROPORTIONATELY, THE EARTH'S CRUST IS ABOUT THE SAME THICKNESS IN RATIO TO ITS MASS AS AN EGG-SHELL IS TO AN EGG.

Today is National Day in New Zealand, where human beings are outnumbered by sheep by about twenty to one.

DURING THE MIDDLE OF THE NINETEENTH CENTURY AN ESTIMATED MILLION AND A HALF IRISH PEOPLE DIED DURING THE POTATO FAMINE.

7

The Beatles made their first visit to America in 1964, arriving on February 7. When they appeared on the popular *Ed Sullivan Show* **the nation's youth were so captivated that during the run of the show hardly any juvenile crimes were committed throughout the whole of the U.S.A.**

Probably the most famous baseball player of all time, Babe Ruth, was born on 7 February 1894. During his career he hit 714 home runs, which remained a record for the next thirty-nine years. He was also one of the highest earning sportsmen of his generation, making a million dollars from his salaries and another million from advertising and public appearances.

February

8

One of the very few man-made objects visible from space is the Great Wall of China.

The Confederate states of America were joined together on 8 February 1861. But throughout the whole of the war that followed they maintained trading links with the Union. The Confederacy was rich in cotton, but low in opium for the wounded, while the Union had plenty of opium but hardly any cotton with which to clothe its forces.

TODAY IS A PUBLIC HOLIDAY IN IRAQ, THE COUNTRY THAT PRODUCES 80 PER CENT OF THE WORLD'S DATES FROM 35,000,000 PALM TREES.

On 8 February 1587, Mary Queen of Scots was executed. Apparently, she was a skilful billiards player.

EVERY WEEK AROUND 9,334,595 PINTS (1,166,824 GALLONS) OF CARLING BLACK LABEL ARE DRUNK IN ENGLAND AND WALES.

Eight of the fifty U.S. states account for 50 per cent of the total U.S. population. The states are California, Illinois, Pennsylvania, Michigan, New Jersey, New York, Texas and Ohio.

9

Today is the feast day of St. Apollonia, the patron saint of toothache sufferers. Official figures show that 97 per cent of children in the U.S.A. suffer from some sort of tooth decay, while in England and Wales dentists remove 4 tons of decayed teeth from childrens' mouths every year.

THE CASHEW NUT IS A MEMBER OF THE SAME FAMILY AS POISON IVY.

Flamingoes can only eat when their heads are upside down.

25

February

10

Upper and Lower Canada were united on 10 February 1840. An old law in the western Canadian province of British Columbia ruled that anyone who attended a symphony concert could be placed in the stocks for three hours.

Queen Victoria and Prince Albert were married on 10 February 1840. The Queen was a carrier of classic haemophilia, a disease that can only be passed to male children and which prevents blood from clotting.

THE CORRECT WAY OF DESCRIBING SEVERAL BARRAGE BALLOONS IS TO CALL THEM A BALLOON BARRAGE.

One great Russian writer, Alexander Pushkin, died on 10 February 1837, and another, Boris Pasternak, was born on 10 February 1890.

11

The Russo-Japanese War of 1904-5 was probably the first war in history in which more men died in battle than died of disease in camp.

Today is National Foundation Day in Japan. One Japanese beach provides bathers with a natural sauna. Steam rises from an underground volcano and Japanese visitors cover themselves with sand to create the right conditions for their seaside sauna.

THE AINU WOMEN OF JAPAN ALWAYS COVER THEIR MOUTHS WITH ONE HAND WHENEVER THEY SPEAK TO MEN.

Special troops were employed in the medieval Japanese armies to count the number of decapitated enemy heads after every battle.

ONLY THE IMPERIAL FAMILY IN JAPAN IS ALLOWED TO DRIVE IN A MAROON-COLOURED CAR.

February

12 Lady Jane Grey, Queen of England for only 13 days, was executed on 12 February 1554. Every English queen named Jane has either died young, been dethroned, gone mad, been imprisoned or been murdered.

Charles Darwin, the scientist who revolutionised the understanding of evolution, was born on 12 February 1809. One of Darwin's more way-out theories put forward the idea that humans were less hairy than apes because of man's increasing preference for women without body hair.

ANYONE WITH AN I.Q. OF 180 OR ABOVE IS LITERALLY ONE IN A MILLION.

Abraham Lincoln, the first U.S. president to be assassinated, was born on the same day as Darwin. During the Civil War he had to refuse a generous offer of help from the King of Siam. The King offered to ship a detachment of war elephants across the Pacific to aid the Union forces.

13 Captain Cook was murdered on 13 February 1779, by natives who realised that he wasn't a god, as they had previously imagined. Six years earlier Cook had presented a tortoise to the King of Tonga. The tortoise outlived both the donor and recipient and died in 1966 when over 200 years old.

Richard Wagner, the master of German opera, died on 13 February 1883. He was the son-in-law of another famous composer, the Hungarian Franz Liszt.

THE SILKWORM ISN'T A WORM. STRICTLY SPEAKING IT'S A CATERPILLAR.

Man dies quicker from lack of sleep than from lack of food.

SNAKES HEAR WITH THEIR TONGUES. THESE ARE SO SENSITIVE THAT THEY CAN DETECT SOUND WAVES.

27

February

14 Oregon achieved its statehood on St. Valentine's Day 1859. A horseshoe found embedded in a tree in Salem, Oregon was completely free of rust when it was extracted, even though it had been inside the tree for a century.

Another U.S. state, Arizona, also became a fully-fledged state on 14 February in 1912. Camels were still being used there in 1870 and it is still against the law to hunt them in Arizona.

AN OWL CAN TURN ITS HEAD RIGHT THE WAY ROUND FROM ONE SIDE TO THE OTHER, THROUGH 360 DEGREES.

Leaves on eucalyptus trees hang vertically.

YOU CAN NEVER SEE A GAGGLE OF GEESE ON THE WING. WHEN THEY ARE FLYING, GEESE ARE CALLED A SKEIN.

15 One of the foremost medieval astronomers, Galileo Galilei, was born on 15 February 1564. His telescope, with which he made many of his most famous discoveries about the stars and planets, was used to open a scientific exhibition in Chicago in 1933. Light from the moon was passed through the telescope and photoelectric cells converted it to power to switch on the lights.

King George VI was buried on 15 February 1952. He was the only King of England ever to bring a future British monarch into the world in a private house with a street number. Queen Elizabeth II was born at 17 Bruton Street, London W1.

THE DEAD OUTNUMBER THE LIVING BY ABOUT THIRTY TO ONE.

February

16

Fidel Castro became Prime Minister of Cuba on 16 February 1959. There are special farms on Cuba that breed an unusual form of livestock - crocodiles.

About 13,000,000 working days are lost in Britain every year as a result of backache.

ON 16 FEBRUARY 1568, THE ENTIRE POPULATION OF THE NETHERLANDS WAS CONDEMNED TO DEATH BY THE SPANISH INQUISITION.

On 16 February 1949, Dr Chaim Weizman was elected first president of Israel. On the night that the United Nations voted to establish the state of Israel, the Dead Sea Scrolls were translated for the first time.

17

The leader of the Apache Indians, Geronimo, who terrorized the southwest of the U.S.A. during the 1880's, died on 17 February 1909, having spent his declining years selling photographs of himself at 25 cents each.

Today is also the feast day of Saint Fintan of Cloneenagh, an Irish monk who lived with a band of others on a diet of stale barley bread and muddy water, with only vegetables to provide a touch of luxury in their lives.

THE ONLY FOOD THAT IS NATURALLY BLUE IS THE IRISH BILBERRY.

Albert I, King of the Belgians, died on 17 February 1934. The Belgian hare is not a hare at all. It's a rabbit.

29

February

18 John Bunyan's *Pilgrim's Progress* was published on 18 February 1678. The author had written most of it while serving a six month prison sentence in Bedford gaol.

The famous Italian artist, Michelangelo Buonarroti, died on 18 February 1564, leaving behind some of the most well-known masterpieces in the world. Not everyone appreciated his work however. Pope Paul IV was so appalled by the naked figures that Michelangelo had painted in his Last Judgement *that he paid another painter to 'clothe' them.*

GARLIC BELONGS TO THE SAME FAMILY AS THE LILY.

On 18 February 1951, the King of Nepal declared that his country was going to be a constitutional monarchy. Nepal is the only Hindu kingdom in the world.

A CAMEL'S BACKBONE IS PERFECTLY STRAIGHT.

Crocusses have been known to grow up through tarmac.

19 The Polish astronomer, Nicholas Copernicus, was born on 19 February 1473. Copernicus established the modern theories about the relationships between the sun and the planets. He also maintained that the stars showed small shifts in their positions as an observer's own position moved. However, it was not possible to measure and confirm these ideas in the Middle Ages. But three centuries after Copernicus died his ideas were proved to be perfectly correct.

The four elements from which medieval philosophers believed that the earth and all matter sprang; earth, air, fire and water, are not elements at all. They are compounds.

THE HUMAN BRAIN IS MORE WATERY THAN HUMAN
BLOOD.

February

20 U.S. astronaut, John Glenn, splashed into the sea and became the first American to fly in space on 20 February 1962. When he was given a hero's welcome in New York City, the people tipped an estimated 3,474 tons of paper on to him in the ticker-tape parade.

Robert Peary, the American explorer, who was credited with being the first man to reach the North Pole, died on 20 February 1920. Getting there alone presents a problem to navigators using conventional compasses. Magnetic north lies some 1,500 miles to the west of the North Pole.

THE NORTH POLE IS MORE THAN 9,000 FEET LOWER THAN THE SOUTH POLE.

Solder, which is formed from lead and tin, melts at 356°F. However, tin melts at 446°F and lead melts at 620°F.

IT TAKES 120 DROPS OF WATER TO FILL A TEASPOON.

21 Today is International Youth Day of Struggle against Colonialism, celebrated in the U.S.S.R. and eastern Europe. The struggle takes many forms, though as yet no one has seriously considered invading the U.S.A., which wouldn't be that difficult, since at their nearest points the two super-powers are less than two miles apart.

The U.S.S.R. is the world's largest consumer of perfume.

ALMOST 40 PER CENT OF THE U.S.S.R. IS COVERED WITH FORESTS.

The Mangrove is one of the very few trees that can grow in salt water.

February

22 George Washington was born on 22 February 1732. Although Washington himself was revered and honoured in his lifetime and after his death, his mother, Mary Washington, did not receive her due recognition until 1894, when a statue was erected to her memory in Fredericksburg, Virginia. This was the first monument paid for by women to honour a woman.

Washington suffered from his teeth throughout his life. He had many sets of dentures, but he always soaked them in port at night to improve their taste.

INSTEAD OF CARRYING A POCKET WATCH, GEORGE WASHINGTON OFTEN WENT ABOUT WITH A PORTABLE SUN-DIAL WITH WHICH HE TOLD THE TIME.

23 John Keats, who worked as a dresser in Guy's Hospital, as well as being one of the best known romantic poets, was born on 23 February 1821.

Samuel Pepys, the famous diarist, was born on 23 February 1633. When he was appointed secretary to the Navy Board, he knew nothing about the Navy and nothing about arithmetic, so he started to learn all he could, which included committing multiplication tables to memory at the age of thirty.

ONLY HARD-BOILED EGGS CAN BE SPUN.

Among the many Americans that died at the Siege of the Alamo on 23 February 1836, was the legendary frontiersman, Davy Crockett.

February

24 The Holy Roman Emperor Charles V was born on 23 February 1500. Lord of Spain, the Netherlands and Germany, he was asked which languages he spoke. 'I speak Spanish to God, Italian to women, French to men, and German to my horse', the emperor replied.

Today is St. Matthias's Day. The saint's namesake, King Matthias Corvinus of Hungary, once ordered all the ladies at his court to sit in his presence; the reasoning being that as they were so ugly he wouldn't have to see as much of them if they were sitting.

THERE ARE TWENTY-SIX COUNTRIES ON EARTH WITH NO COASTLINE AT ALL.

Buttermilk doesn't actually contain any butter, since all the butter fat has been removed by that stage.

IN THE BEST AGRICULTURAL CONDITIONS CEREALS PRODUCE DOUBLE THE AMOUNT OF CALORIES PRODUCED BY DAIRY FARMING.

There are approximately four babies born every second, which gives an hourly total of 14,400.

25 25 February wasn't a good day for Queen Elizabeth I. On 25 February 1570 Pope Pius V excommunicated her and declared her a usurper, and thirty-one years later, her favourite the Earl of Essex, was executed.

Queen Elizabeth I was the only British sovereign between the Norman conquest and the present day who did not effectively possess any land outside England and Wales.

TESTS HAVE SHOWN THAT MOSQUITOS PREFER BLONDES.

After she lost her teeth, Queen Elizabeth I never appeared in public without first padding out her mouth with wads of cotton to improve her appearance.

33

February

26 The Second French Republic was proclaimed on 26 February 1848. If all the wine corks used to stop bottles of French wine each year were laid end to end, they would form a chain that could encircle the world ten times.

William F. Cody was born on 26 February 1846. He became better known as Buffalo Bill, although he actually hunted bison.

IN THE HISTORY OF THE WORLD THERE HAVE BEEN TEN YEARS OF WAR FOR EVERY YEAR OF PEACE.

Sir Christopher Wren, who died on 26 February 1723, only received £200 a year while he was supervising the construction of St. Paul's Cathedral.

THE WOOD OF THE HORNBEAM IS USUALLY USED TO MAKE PIANO KEYS.

27 The American poet, Henry Wadsworth Longfellow, was born on 17 February 1807. In writing his most well-known poem, *The Song of Hiawatha*, he used the metre of a Finnish epic poem called the *Kalevala*.

The first Russian trade mission to England arrived in London on 27 February 1558. Today Russia produces enough coal in one year to power London's electricity supply for over 100 years.

MAN IS THE ONLY ANIMAL THAT SLEEPS ON ITS BACK.

The diarist, John Evelyn, was born on 26 February 1706, the grandson of the first man ever to build gunpowder mills in England.

THERE ARE NEARLY THREE AND HALF TIMES AS MANY COUNTRIES NORTH OF THE EQUATOR AS THERE ARE COUNTRIES TO THE SOUTH OF IT.

Between 1500 and 1600 the stock of precious metals in Europe trebled.

February

28 King Christian IV of Denmark died on 28 February 1648. The Danish national flag is one of the oldest in the world. The white cross set against a red background was adopted in 1219.

King Alfonso XIII also died on 28 February, though in his case it was in 1941. He was King of Spain, a country that took its name from a Carthaginian word that meant 'Land of Rabbits'.

THE SAILFISH IS CAPABLE OF SWIMMING FASTER THAN A HORSE CAN GALLOP.

One of the greatest English novels, The History of Tom Jones, A Foundling, *was published on 28 February 1749. Its author, Henry Fielding was paid £700 for it.*

IN THE LATE SEVENTEENTH CENTURY, 'TEA' WAS PRONOUNCED 'TAY'.

29 Gioacchino Rossini, the composer of some of the most popular operas ever written, was born on 29 February 1792. He completed the score of one of his most successful works, *The Barber of Seville,* in only eight days.

Rossini had little time for composers who excused their paltry efforts on the grounds that there were no worthwhile subjects to stimulate their creative powers. He used to tell them: "Give me a laundry list and I'll set it to music".

ALTOGETHER ROSSINI WROTE 38 OPERAS IN THE FIRST 37 YEARS OF HIS LIFE. HOWEVER, HE WROTE NO MORE AFTER THAT, EVEN THOUGH HE LIVED FOR ANOTHER 39 YEARS.

Frogs' tongues grow from the front of their mouths. This gives them a longer reach for catching insects.

EUNUCHS HAVE ONE BIG ADVANTAGE OVER OTHERS. THEY DO NOT SUFFER FROM ADOLESCENT ACNE.

March

I **Ohio achieved its statehood on St. David's Day, 1803. A law in the state requires domestic animals to wear tail-lights if they are out after lighting-up time.**

MOST OF US MOVE AT LEAST FORTY TIMES IN OUR SLEEP, INSOMNIACS MAY MOVE AS MANY AS SEVENTY TIMES.

On 1 March 1950, Chiang Kai-Shek resumed the presidency of Nationalist China (Taiwan). Today Taiwan is a world leader in the export of mushrooms.

ZEBRAS HAVE WHITE STRIPES, NOT BLACK ONES.

On average we each consume about one ton of food and drink every year.

THE MURDER RATE IN MEDIEVAL ENGLAND WAS ABOUT TWENTY-SIX TIMES GREATER THAN IT IS TODAY.

Lumps of ice, well insulated in glass fibre, have been baked in oven temperatures of 190°C without melting.

THE RHINOCEROS HAS A GESTATION PERIOD OF 560 DAYS.

Ostriches can run at speeds of up to 40 mph and in South Africa there are ostrich races in which ostriches carrying jockeys race against each other.

March

○○○○○○○○○○○○○○○○○○○○○○○○○○○○○○○○○

2

Independence was restored to Morocco on 2 March 1956. Moroccan men can restore their own independence very easily. To get a divorce, all a man has to do is to tell his wife 'I divorce you' three times.

The Republic of Texas was founded by a group of 59 Mexican citizens on 2 March 1836. Today the state of Texas has 254 counties. Alaska, which is twice the size of Texas, hasn't any counties at all.

ONE 75-WATT BULB PRODUCES MORE LIGHT THAN THREE 25-WATT BULBS.

The people of Luxembourg drink two and a half times as much beer as they drink wine, and today is a bank holiday in Luxembourg.

IT TAKES A CORK TREE OVER TEN YEARS TO GROW ONE LAYER OF CORK.

It was less than a century ago that the practice of storing corpses awaiting burial, in pub cellars, came to an end.

○○○○○○○○○○○○○○○○○○○○○○○○○○○○○○○○○

3

In 1966 one 17-year-old Florida girl started to sneeze at the beginning of January and didn't stop until six months later.

Florida became a proper U.S. state on 3 March 1845. One popular hors d'oeuvre served in the state is rattlesnake meat.

WE USE 17 MUSCLES TO SMILE AND 43 TO FROWN.

Today is the Feast of Dolls in Japan. In Japanese puppet theatres, the puppets are manipulated in full view of the audience.

WHEN FLIES TAKE OFF THEY START WITH A BACKWARD JUMP.

March

4

On 4 March 1681, William Penn was granted a patent for territory in North America by King Charles II. Penn founded Pennsylvania, but his schemes ranged wider still. He had the idea of establishing an organization like the United Nations, two and half centuries before it was established.

David Rice Atchison became president of the U.S.A. for one day on 4 March 1849. One president's term of office had come to an end, his successor would not be sworn in on a Sunday, so Atchison, the president of the Senate, became acting president for a day.

EVERY TENTH EGG IS LARGER THAN THE NINE LAID BEFORE IT.

The ancient Greeks used to believe that the womb was divided into two compartments with the boys coming from the right-hand one and the girls coming from the left-hand one.

5

King James I died on 5 March 1625. Among the sports and pastimes thought unsuitable for Sunday during his reign were : bear-baiting, short plays and mimes and bowling.

The terror of Russia in the 1930's, Joseph Stalin, died on 5 March 1953. Although he was always seen in public smoking a pipe, Stalin was a chain-smoker of cigarettes in private life.

BEFORE ENTERING POLITICS, JOSEPH STALIN HAD BEEN STUDYING THEOLOGY WITH THE IDEA OF JOINING THE PRIESTHOOD.

The word 'tap' has the same meaning as the word formed by reversing the order of the letters, 'pat'.

VINTAGE PORT TAKES 40 YEARS TO REACH ITS PROPER MATURITY.

March

Michelangelo, who was born on 6 March 1475, occasionally made mistakes in his works. His famous statue of Moses shows the leader of the children of Israel with horns protruding from his head. Unfortunately a translation error that confused the Hebrew words for 'Horn' and 'Ray of Light' led Michelangelo and other artists astray.

The first packaged frozen foods appeared in shops on 6 March 1930. These were the brainchild of Clarence Birdseye, who had developed the technique after watching Eskimo's catching fish in temperatures of -50°F, which froze them solid almost as soon as they came out of the water.

SINGING CHRISTMAS CAROLS WAS BANNED BY THE PURITANS.

Basking sharks have livers that are so large that they often account for 10 per cent of the fish's body weight.

Alexander Graham Bell patented his first telephone on 7 March 1876. The telephone had originally been invented during research into a hearing aid.

The composer of the Bolero, Maurice Ravel, was born on 7 March 1875. He referred to this, his most famous work, as "seventeen minutes of orchestra without any music". The same eight-measure theme is repeated in different forms by the orchestra for the entire piece.

ESKIMOS USUALLY USE THEIR REFRIGERATORS TO PREVENT THEIR FOOD FROM FREEZING.

The famous Korean genius, Ki, was born on 7 March 1963. He wasn't five years old by the time he could speak four languages and understand integral calculus. His I.Q., the highest ever recorded, has been given as 210!

March

America's largest president, William Howard Taft, died on 8 March 1930. Taft was so large that a special bath had to be installed for him in the White House. This bath was so big that four of the workmen installing it were able to climb inside and have their photograph taken.

William Howard Taft was also the only man ever to be both Chief Justice and President of the U.S.A.

TODAY THERE ARE MORE THAN 28,000,000 CATS IN THE U.S.A.

On 8 March 1844, King Charles XIV of Sweden died. By then his nation were getting a taste for coffee; a taste which has led them to become the world's greatest coffee drinkers. Today Sweden consumes the equivalent of over 29 lbs of coffee per inhabitant every year.

THERE ARE MORE THAN TWENTY WORDS FOR 'SNOW' IN THE ESKIMO LANGUAGE.

On 9 March 1451, an explorer was born, whose name was to become more of a household word than that of any other. His name was Amerigo Vespucci and his christian name was used to name the New World, America. The Italian explorer was the first to discover the mainland of America.

If all the hot dogs made in the U.S.A. every year were joined end to end, they would form a giant hot dog stretching from the earth to the moon and back 2½ times.

TODAY THE U.S.A. HAS LESS THAN ONE SIXTH OF THE TOTAL WORLD POPULATION AND YET IT CONSUMES ALMOST THREE FIFTHS OF THE EARTH'S TOTAL RESOURCES.

March

10

Henry Fowler, one of the leading authorities ever on the English language, and the author of *Modern English Usage*, was born on 10 March 1858. The English language contains nearly 800,000 words and technical terms, which is more than in any other language.

There is only one word in English that is pronounced exactly the same way when the last four letters are taken away. The word is 'queue'.

'E' IS THE MOST COMMONLY USED LETTER IN ENGLISH, THE ONE USED LEAST IS 'Q'.

Spelled backwards, the word 'live' is 'evil'.

SKIPPING USES UP TWICE AS MANY CALORIES AS MAKING LOVE.

Ants and termites have been known to burrow to a depth of eighty feet, in search of water.

THE AVERAGE ICEBERG WEIGHS TWENTY MILLION TONS.

☽☽☽☽☽☽☽☽☽☽☽☽☽☽☽☽☽☽☽☽☽☽☽☽☽☽☽☽

11

The first victim of a railway accident, William Huskisson, was born today. His birthday was 11 March 1770. Huskisson was run over by Stevenson's engine on the opening run of the Liverpool to Manchester railway line. He is commemorated by a six foot high statue, clad in a Roman toga.

Most of the sensations that we know as tastes are really smells.

THE ONLY ANIMAL WITH FOUR KNEES IS AN ELEPHANT.

Ferrets can catch colds in the same way as humans catch them.

March

12 The Indian Ocean island of Mauritius became independent on 12 March 1968. Until 1681 Mauritius had been the home of the giant pigeon called the dodo. However, visiting sailors in search of fresh meat killed off the dodos and by 1681 they were extinct.

The first ballet tutu made its appearance at the premiere of Les Sylphides *on 12 March 1832. It caused an uproar as the audience could see the dancers' ankles, and their arms exposed to the shoulders.*

IT TAKES A TON OF COAL TO MAKE THE SAME WEIGHT OF PAPER.

On 12 March 1938, German troops entered Austria. In Upper Austria there is an island on Lake Alm that is constantly moving from one shore to the other.

MINUS 40°C IS THE SAME TEMPERATURE AS MINUS 40°F.

☙☙☙☙☙☙☙☙☙☙☙☙☙☙☙☙☙☙☙☙☙☙☙☙☙☙☙☙

13 The discovery of two new planets was announced on 13 March. In 1781, Sir William Herschel discovered the planet Uranus and in 1930 it was announced that Pluto had been discovered.

Halley's comet came to its perihelion (the point at which it is nearest to the sun) on 13 March 1758. Halley had predicted this very event in 1682, seventy-three years earlier.

URANUS TAKES 84 YEARS TO ORBIT THE SUN.

Pluto's only moon is no more than 12,000 miles from the surface of the planet, and because its orbit is the same as that of the planet, it would always appear in the same place to anyone who was looking at it night after night.

IF YOU WERE STANDING ON THE SURFACE OF PLUTO AND LOOKING AT THE SUN, IT WOULDN'T APPEAR ANY BRIGHTER THAN VENUS APPEARS IN OUR EVENING SKY.

March

14

Albert Einstein, the father of atomic theory, was born in Ulm, in southern Germany, on 14 March 1879. He must have been something of a late developer since he failed to pass the entrance examinations for the Federal Polytechnic of Zurich when he was a young man.

Among his peculiarities, Einstein hated wearing socks and never used shaving soap. He shaved with a razor and warm water.

AN EQUALLY INFLUENTIAL FIGURE, KARL MARX, DIED ON 14 MARCH 1884. DURING ONE STAGE IN HIS LIFE HE HAD WORKED AS A JOURNALIST IN LONDON.

On 14 March 1903, the Civil Service Gazette *suggested that a bottle of Bass was "...something reviving when one is a little out of sorts, something one can fly to with a distinct relish when the morning brings an awakening to overnight discretions..." In other words it was an ideal cure for civil service hangovers.*

15

Julius Caesar was murdered on the Ides of March (15 March) 44 BC. Experts have placed a value of over £1,000,000 on his autograph.

In later life Julius Caesar became totally bald and to hide this he always appeared in public wearing a laurel wreath on his head.

HUMAN MUSCLES ALWAYS WORK BY PULLING. THEY NEVER PUSH.

The state of Maine was incorporated into the U.S.A. on 15 March 1820. Casco Bay in Maine has exactly 365 islands, suitably named the Calendar Islands.

SILKWORMS ARE CAPABLE OF CONSUMING 86,000 TIMES THEIR BODY WEIGHT IN ONLY 56 DAYS.

One study into the common cold revealed that people were more likely to catch colds when their mothers-in-law came to stay.

March

16

There is a copper mine in the city of Falun, in Sweden, that has been mining copper for the same company for over 700 years.

The right to pick mushrooms is protected by law in Sweden. Every Swede is allowed access to the forests where they grow.

RED SQUIRRELS ATTRACT MORE FLEAS THAN ANY OTHER ANIMAL.

The American Military Academy was established at West Point on 16 March 1802. Among its less august entrants was the artist James Whistler. He failed his exams with great style however. Asked by one examiner how he would explain his ignorance of the date of an important battle, if he were asked it at dinner, Whistler answered that he would never associate with people who discussed such things at the table.

17

Today is St. Patrick's Day, and a public holiday in Ireland. Although he is patron saint of Ireland, St. Patrick was born on the west coast of Britain, and only went to Ireland when he was kidnapped by pirates.

Another curiosity about the Irish saint is that St.Patrick's Cathedral in Dublin is not a catholic church, it is protestant.

THE GALLANT CAPTAIN OATES WAS BOTH BORN AND DIED ON 17 MARCH. HE WAS BORN IN 1880, AND THIRTY-TWO YEARS LATER HE WALKED OUT OF SCOTT'S TENT TO DISAPPEAR IN AN ANTARCTIC BLIZZARD IN A DESPERATE EFFORT TO SAVE HIS FRIENDS.

The Irish drink more tea per person than any other nation in the world.

March

18 Revolution broke out in Milan on 18 March 1848. Milan Cathedral took 579 years to build and can seat a congregation of 40,000.

The Tsar of Russia, Ivan the Terrible, was born on 18 March 1584. When he wished to marry he ordered all the nobles in his realm to send their daughters of marriageable age to Moscow. Any noble who refused faced execution, so some 1,500 girls arrived. After inspecting each one, Ivan chose his bride. This process was so successful that he used it with his two subsequent marriages.

CLOUDS FLY HIGHER DURING THE DAY THAN THEY DO AT NIGHT.

Stephen Grover Cleveland, the only U.S. President to be married in the White House, was born on 18 March 1837. His other claim to fame is as a draft dodger. In order to avoid conscription, he hired another man to take his place in the forces.

THE DOORMOUSE SPENDS ABOUT SIX MONTHS OF EVERY YEAR HIBERNATING.

19 The great Victorian traveller, Sir Richard Burton, was born on 19 March 1821. Apart from being the most travelled man of his age, he was also the first westerner ever to penetrate the holy Muslim city of Mecca. He could speak twenty languages and he was one of the first white men to sail down the Amazon.

The volume of water in the River Amazon is greater than the combined total of the next eight largest rivers on earth.

THE DAILY OUTFLOW FROM THE AMAZON WOULD BE ENOUGH TO SUPPLY THE U.S.A. WITH ITS MUNICIPAL WATER REQUIREMENT FOR TWO HUNDRED DAYS.

In a churchyard near Oaxara, in Mexico, stands an ahuehuete tree that measures 160 feet in circumference and that is believed to be one of the oldest living things on the whole American continent.

45

March

20 Sir Isaac Newton died on 20 March 1727. His only recorded utterance as a member of Parliament was a request that a window should be opened.

In 1687 Newton published his Mathematical Principles of Natural Philosophy, *in which he put forward the idea of using man-made satellites in outer space.*

HUMMINGBIRDS MAKE THEIR CHARACTERISTIC HUMMING SOUND BY BEATING THEIR WINGS.

Almost all the fish caught in the world come from the waters over the continental shelves. However, these constitute less than ten per cent of the area of the oceans.

21 Today is the birthday of the famous Mexican revolutionary, Benito Juarez, who was born on 21 March 1806, and consequently it's a public holiday in Mexico. Today there are still over fifty groups of pure Indians living in Mexico, each with its own distinct language and culture.

THERE IS A STREET IN GUANAJUAT, IN MEXICO, THAT IS SO NARROW THAT SWEETHEARTS CAN LEAN ACROSS FROM OPPOSITE BALCONIES AND KISS EACH OTHER.

The poet, Robert Southey, died on 21 March 1843. His magazine from Westminster School, The Flagellant, *has the unique distinction among school magazines of being confined to the restricted case in the British Museum.*

JOHANN SEBASTIAN BACH WAS BORN ON 21 MARCH 1685. HE WASN'T THE ONLY MUSICIAN IN HIS FAMILY BY ANY MEANS. THERE WERE OVER FIFTY OTHERS.

March

22 **Johann Wolfgang Von Goethe, the German poet and philosopher, died on 22 March 1832. When he was barely ten years old, he wrote a story in seven languages.**

The famous Dutch painter, Sir Anthony Van Dyck, was born on 22 March 1599. He is probably best known for his paintings of Charles I. However, in one of these he painted the king dressed in full armour and carrying two gauntlets. The only problem with the painting is that both gauntlets are for the right hand.

HUSBANDS WERE NOT ALLOWED TO BEAT THEIR WIVES AFTER 10 PM IN SIXTEENTH CENTURY BRITAIN.

A female cicada can hear her mate calling when they are a mile apart.

◦◦◦◦◦◦◦◦◦◦◦◦◦◦◦◦◦◦◦◦◦◦◦◦◦◦◦◦◦◦◦◦

23 **On 23 March 1848, the first officially organised band of settlers landed at Dunedin, in New Zealand. One of the first settlers in New Zealand, Henry Burling, lived to be over 100 years old, and left 600 descendants when he died.**

The earth's crust is so thin in some parts of New Zealand that pools of boiling mud bubble on the surface, fed by hot springs and steam that rise from the molten rocks not far from the surface.

THE KIWI, THE NATIONAL BIRD OF NEW ZEALAND, HAS A BEAK THAT IS SO SENSITIVE THAT IT CAN DETECT WORMS DEEP IN THE GROUND.

The Maoris of New Zealand used to regard tattoos on the chin as a sign of high rank. Although the practice no longer exists, it is still quite common to see it among older Maoris.

THE TUATARA LIZARD THAT IS FOUND IN NEW ZEALAND IS A LIVING FOSSIL. IT IS THE LAST SURVIVOR OF AN ORDER OF REPTILES THAT WERE COMMON 250,000,000 YEARS AGO.

March

Queen Elizabeth I died on 24 March 1603. Twenty-eight years before, she had been offered the sovereignty of the Netherlands, but had turned it down.

King James I acceded to the English throne on the day on which Queen Elizabeth I died. He was one of only three British sovereigns who were left-handed. The others were, George IV and Queen Victoria.

AFTER HER DEATH, IT WAS DISCOVERED THAT QUEEN ELIZABETH I HAD 2,000 GOWNS IN HER WARDROBE.

When the M5 was being constructed near Exeter, a special underpass, measuring only one foot in diameter, was built under the road. It is designed to help badgers cross the motorway.

25

Greece became independent on 25 March 1924 and was proclaimed a republic. Today is a Greek national holiday. Even though 75 per cent of the country is mountainous, rocky and barren, 60 per cent of the population make their living from agriculture.

Until 1751, today had always been New Year's Day, but the Julian calendar which was being used was losing time at the rate of three days in every 400 years and things had got seriously out of control. So in 1751 the government switched to the Gregorian calendar and today became 5 April.

THE INDIAN ATLAS MOTH HAS A WING SPAN OF 11 INCHES.

The fiery Italian conductor, Arturo Toscanini, was born in Parma on 25 March 1867. At one time he stood for election to the Italian Parliament, as a fascist candidate.

RAINBOWS ONLY OCCUR WHEN THE SUN IS BELOW AN ANGLE OF 40° ABOVE THE HORIZON.

March

The great actress Sarah Bernhardt died on 26 March 1923. In her later years she often appeared on stage wearing a wooden leg, and when news leaked out that she had had a leg amputated she received a request from an American businessman to display her leg in San Francisco. She replied asking which leg he had in mind.

Another great figure of the English stage, Noel Coward, also died on 26 March, in 1973. He wrote one of his most popular plays 'Hay Fever' in only three days.

THE MOST DANGEROUS FIRES FACED BY FIREMEN ARE THOSE IN WHICH EITHER CORK OR RUBBER ARE BURNING.

Ducks only lay eggs in the early morning.

27

The English novelist, Arnold Bennett, died in Paris on 27 March 1931 under tragic, if ridiculous circumstances. He died of typhoid contracted from drinking a glass of local water in an attempt to prove that Parisian water was quite safe to drink.

King James I died on 27 March 1625. Among his many writings, the king had launched a broadside against the habit of smoking, which was still in its infancy at the beginning of the seventeenth century. 'Smoking is a custom loathsome to the eye, hateful to the nose, harmful to the brain, dangerous to the lungs', wrote the king over three and a half centuries ago.

DURING THE BOER WAR, IN 1899, A SET OF BOER KIT WAS FOUND. APART FROM THE USUAL RIFLE, BANDOLIER AND WATER BOTTLE, THE BOER QUARTERMASTER HAD THOUGHTFULLY PROVIDED A BOTTLE OF BASS.

March

○○○○○○○○○○○○○○○○○○○○○○○○○○○○○○○○○○

 The world went up for auction on 28 March 193 AD. Following the assassination of the emperor, Pertinax, the Praetorian Guard offered the Empire (i.e. the world) to the highest bidder. The lucky man had the lot knocked down for just under £20,000,000, and promptly called himself Emperor Julianus. However, sixty-six days later he was knocked down himself and the Emperor Septimus Severus took over. It didn't cost him a penny.

One of the twentieth centuries greatest female writers, Virginia Woolf, died on 28 March 1941. During her younger days she had once taken part in an elaborate practical joke in which a group of Cambridge undergraduates conned the Royal Navy into entertaining them to a formal reception on board a flagship, on the pretext that they were none other than the Emperor of Ethiopia and his entourage. The Navy swallowed the hoax hook, line and sinker.

ANOTHER WORLD FAMOUS RULER APPEARED ON THE SCENE TODAY. KING GEORGE I OF ENGLAND WAS BORN IN GERMANY ON 28 MARCH 1660. IN SPITE OF REIGNING IN ENGLAND FOR THIRTEEN YEARS, THE KING COULDN'T SPEAK ENGLISH.

○○○○○○○○○○○○○○○○○○○○○○○○○○○○○○○○○○

 Captain Scott wrote the final words in his diary, in his tent in Antarctica, on 29 March 1912. When he and his two companions died they were only eleven miles from the food and fuel that would have saved them.

The battle of Towton in Yorkshire (just off the A1 between Ferrybridge and Tadcaster) was fought on 29 March 1461. Not only was this the bloodiest battle ever fought in the Wars of the Roses, but it was also the bloodiest ever fought in Britain. A total of 76,000 men clashed on that day, and when the sun set as many as 38,000 lay dead on the field.

A GOOSE WILL REMAIN FAITHFUL TO HER GANDER ALL HER LIFE.

March

30 The U.S.A. made one of its most important purchases today. On 30 March 1867, it bought Alaska from Russia. The purchase price was $7,200,000 which worked out at about 2 cents per acre.

THE HUSBAND OF THE FEMALE ANGLER FISH IS SO MUCH SMALLER THAN HIS WIFE THAT SHE CARRIES HIM ALONG ATTACHED TO HER UNDERSIDE.

The Alaskan coastline is longer than the total coastline of the other forty-eight states of the American continent.

HOT WATER IS HEAVIER THAN COLD WATER.

Grasshoppers have white blood.

THERE ARE STILL ACTIVE VOLCANOES IN ALASKA.

Billiard tables didn't have rubber cushions until 1835 and slate beds didn't appear until the following year.

IRON NAILS SHOULD NEVER BE USED IN OAK BECAUSE AN ACID IN THE WOOD CORRODES IRON.

31 Francis I, King of France, died on the last day of March 1547. During his reign he had banned the wearing of whiskers. Anyone found with a beard or a moustache in his realm was liable to be put to death.

THE COMMONEST PUB NAME IN ENGLAND IS THE 'RED LION'.

Franz Josef Haydn was born on 31 March 1732. Haydn was a happy, amusing man, who always enjoyed a joke. He even included one or two in his music. In his piano Sonata in A, for example, he composed a minuet in reverse, the second part of which was exactly the same as the first, but played backwards.

April

1

Whether by coincidence or by design both the Royal Air Force and the U.S. Air Force Academy came into being on April Fool's Day. The R.A.F. was formed in 1918, the U.S.A.F. Academy in 1954.

April Fool!

BEARS OFTEN CLIMB TELE-GRAPH POLES IN THEIR SEARCH FOR HONEY. EXPERTS BELIEVE THAT THE HUMMING OF THE WIRES CONFUSES THE BEARS WHICH MISTAKE IT FOR THE HUMMING OF BEES.

Under section 4 of the 1824 Vagrancy Act fortune tellers are still liable to punishment.

IT WAS ONCE ILLEGAL TO HAVE A MIDDLE NAME IN ENGLAND.

When he was still at school, the romantic poet, Thomas Chatterton, taught himself medieval English and then used it to write poems by an imaginary medieval monk. His poems were read by many leading scholars as serious works of literature. Only a hundred years later did the truth emerge.

IT WAS CUSTOMARY IN ANCIENT ROME TO TOAST A LADY BY DRINKING ONE GLASS OF WINE FOR EVERY LETTER OF HER NAME.

The official name for Libya is Splaj. The initials stand for the Socialist People's Libyan Arab Jamahiriya.

April

2

One of France's most famous novelists, Emile Zola, was born on 2 April 1840. Zola's literary promise was not immediately apparent when he was awarded a zero in one examination on French literature and failed German and Rhetoric at school.

Casanova, the last word (or name) in lovers, was born on 2 April 1725. It wasn't uncommon for him to consume fifty oysters for breakfast, presumably to help him maintain his legendary powers.

IF YOU STICK TO LATITUDE 60° SOUTH YOU'LL BE ABLE TO SAIL ALL THE WAY ROUND THE WORLD.

A wren can sing as many as 130 notes in only seven seconds.

3

The first Pony Express rider set out across the U.S.A. on 3 April 1860. In spite of its immense legendary appeal in westerns and U.S. folklore, the service only lasted two years, when Indian raids and the newly invented telegraph put it out of business.

Israel's Arab neighbours declared an armistice with the Jewish state on 3 April 1949. Today Israel is the only country in the world with compulsory military service for women.

GAMEKEEPER'S THUMB IS AN AILMENT OFTEN SUFFERED BY SKIERS.

On 3 April 1798 the Commander-in-chief of the British army, the Duke of York, recalled to active service 'every lieutenant colonel under twenty, and every captain under the age of twelve'.

ANTS CAN PULL LOADS THAT ARE UP TO THREE HUNDRED TIMES THEIR OWN WEIGHT.

The female meadow vole is a remarkable mother. Capable of reproducing only twenty-five days after her own birth, she can give birth to up to seventeen litters a year, each of which consists of six to eight young.

April

4

The North Atlantic Treaty was signed in Washington D.C. on 4 April 1949. The Pentagon, which is the headquarters of the alliance's major contributor, the U.S. armed forces, is the world's largest office building covering an area of six and a half million square feet. It has its own post office, restaurants, bus station and shops.

If you have blue blood it means one of two things: that you are being asphyxiated or that you are a lobster.

5

Two twentieth century British Prime Ministers resigned today. On 5 April 1955, Sir Winston Churchill resigned and twenty-one years later, Sir Harold Wilson also resigned.

PEPSI-COLA WAS ORIGINALLY DEVELOPED AS A CURE FOR HANGOVERS.

Elihu Yale was born on 5 April 1648. Although the famous American university in New Haven now bears his name, it was not founded by him. Indeed, Yale University was originally established as the Collegiate School of Connecticut, by a group of ten men, nine of them from Yale's great rival, Harvard. The name of the university was changed, after Yale made generous donations, in 1718.

6

Richard I, King of England, was killed in battle on 6 April 1199. In spite of reigning for ten years he spent a total of only six months in the country.

The painter Raphael died on 6 April 1520. Eight years later another famous artist, Albrecht Dürer died on the same day. While on 6 April 1826 and 1869, two more artists, Gustave Moreau and Louis Raemaeckers, were born to redress the balance.

April

7

The poet of the Lakes, William Wordsworth, was born on 7 April 1770. For seven years of his life he was Poet Laureate, though in all that time he did not publish a single line of poetry.

Since 560 the cuckoo has traditionally sung first at St. Brynach, in Wales, on 7 April.

THERE IS ENOUGH FAT IN THE AVERAGE HUMAN BODY TO MAKE SEVEN BARS OF SOAP.

On 7 April 1956, Spain relinquished its power in Morocco. Ismail the Bloodthirsty, a former ruler of Morocco was reputedly the father of 548 sons and 340 daughters.

GOLDFISH WILL OFTEN TURN WHITE IF THEY ARE LEFT IN A DARK ROOM FOR A LONG TIME.

8

The twentieth century's most celebrated painter, Pablo Picasso, died on 8 April 1973. His early years as a painter were spent in poverty and obscurity, however. In fact, at times he had to keep himself warm by burning his drawings.

Picasso's full name was Pablo Diego Jose Francisco de Paula Juan Nepomuceno Maria de los Remedios Cipriano de la Santissima Trinidad Ruiz Picasso.

KING PHILIP IV OF SPAIN WAS BORN ON 8 APRIL 1605. HIS LIFE WAS LESS HAPPY THAN PICASSO'S AND HE WAS ONLY REPORTED TO HAVE SMILED THREE TIMES WHEN HE WAS ALIVE.

Six large fireflies produce enough light to read by in the dark.

YOU CAN USUALLY TELL IF A MAN IS LEFT-HANDED OR RIGHT-HANDED BY WATCHING WHICH LEG HE PUTS INTO HIS TROUSERS FIRST.

April

9 The French poet Baudelaire was born on 9 April 1821. When he grew up he became one of the leading nineteenth century French poets and a drug addict.

Isambard Kingdom Brunel, the genius of nineteenth century engineering, was born on 9 April 1806. During his life he designed the Clifton suspension bridge, the tunnel under the Thames from Wapping to Rotherhithe and all the viaducts, bridges and tunnels on the Great Western Railway. He also masterminded the construction of the first wooden steam ship built to cross the Atlantic, the Great Western, the first large iron-hulled screw-driven steam ship, the Great Britain, and the largest ship of his day, the Great Eastern, that laid the first transatlantic telegraph cable.

ABOUT HALF THE PEOPLE ON EARTH LIVE ON A STAPLE DIET OF RICE.

The three-toed sloth is partially disguised by letting its body become covered with tiny plants.

10 The most famous bell in England, Big Ben, was cast on 10 April 1858. The clock which controls the huge bell was once slowed by five minutes in 1945 when so many starlings settled on the minute hand that the whole mechanism was slowed.

On 10 April 1841 the New York (Herald) Tribune was published for the first time. Today nearly half the papers in the world are published in North America.

BY COINCIDENCE ONE OF AMERICA'S MOST FAMOUS JOURNALISTS, JOSEPH PULITZER, WAS BORN ON 10 APRIL 1847. ONE MID-NINETEENTH CENTURY PAPER, PUBLISHED IN THE STATE OF OHIO, MEASURED $7\frac{1}{2}$ FEET LONG BY $5\frac{1}{2}$ FEET WIDE. TWO PEOPLE HAD TO HOLD IT TO BE ABLE TO READ IT.

April

11

On 11 April 1814 Napoleon Bonaparte abdicated. In spite of his many great battles the emperor was terrified of one living creature in particular — the cat.

In his happier days, Napoleon designed the Italian flag.

CASTOR OIL IS ONE OF THE BEST NATURAL LUBRICANTS IN THE WORLD. IT KEEPS ALMOST EVERYTHING RUNNING SMOOTHLY FROM BABIES TO THE MOST SOPHISTICATED JET AIRCRAFT.

It has been known for divers who have been breathing pure oxygen for thirty minutes prior to a descent to be able to hold their breath under water for as long as thirteen minutes.

12

The first major engagement of the American Civil War, the battle of Fort Sumter, began on 12 April 1861. However, it wasn't until nine days after the war began that the first casualties were killed on the battlefield.

During the American Civil War both armies agreed to treat George Washington's house at Mount Vernon, Virginia, as neutral territory and the house was left unharmed by both sides.

THE CONFEDERATE COMMANDER, ROBERT E. LEE, HAD NEVER ACTUALLY COMMANDED AN ARMY IN THE FIELD UNTIL THE OUTBREAK OF THE CIVIL WAR.

The bayonet takes its name from the town of Bayonne, in France.

OVER EIGHTY DIFFERENT VARIETIES OF RICE ARE GROWN IN INDIA.

April

13

The founder of the world's largest chain of department stores, Frank Winfield Woolworth, was born on 13 April 1852. He opened his first shop in 1879 and one hundred years later the Woolworth chain had six thousand shops dotted around the world.

The great American statesman, Thomas Jefferson, was born on 13 April 1743. In his first draft of the American Declaration of Independence he included a clause to abolish slavery. However, popular pressure forced him to delete this.

ONE ANAGRAM OF FUNERAL IS 'REAL FUN'.

Every year the sun burns up an estimated 22 million billion tons of hydrogen.

14

On the night of the 14/15 April 1912 the S.S. *Titanic* hit an iceberg in the Atlantic and sank on her maiden voyage. Fourteen years earlier a novel called *Futility* had been published. In this, the author, Morgan Robertson, had described the collision of a ship with an iceberg in the North Atlantic. The name of his fictitious ship was the *Titan*.

George Frederick Handel died on 14 April 1759. In 1923, 164 years later, the North American publishers of the sheet music of his famous choral work the Messiah, *sued the writers of the song* We have No Bananas *on the grounds that they had taken the melody from Handel's work. The publishers won the case.*

ON 14 APRIL 73 AD, 960 BESIEGED JEWS IN THE FORTRESS OF MASADA KILLED THEMSELVES IN PREFERENCE TO SURRENDERING TO THE ATTACKING ROMAN ARMY.

Dragonflies catch their prey by putting their legs into the shape of a basket.

April

15 On 15 April 1942, King George VI awarded the George Cross to the Mediterranean island of Malta. Maltese is the only Semitic language spoken in Europe.

After killing his opponent and making himself emperor of Rome, Emperor Otho committed suicide three months later as soon as his other rival set foot on Italian soil to challenge him on 15 April 69 AD.

UNLESS YOU ARE HELD UNDERWATER, IT IS IMPOSSIBLE TO DROWN IN THE DEAD SEA BECAUSE IT IS SO SALTY.

The card game, bridge, originated in Turkey.

16 The battle of Culloden was fought on 16 April 1746. It was the last battle fought on British soil.

A reward of 30,000 was offered for the capture of Bonnie Prince Charlie after his defeat at Culloden. However, thanks to Flora MacDonald, it was never claimed.

DOGS CAN HEAR HIGH-FREQUENCY SOUNDS THAT ARE INAUDIBLE TO HUMAN EARS.

The novelist and nobel prize winner, Anatole France, was born on 16 April 1844. His brain was exactly half the size of that of the great Russian novelist, Ivan Turgenev.

THE PENINSULAR OF MOUNT ATHOS IN NORTHERN GREECE IS INHABITED SOLELY BY MONKS. NOTHING FEMALE IS ALLOWED ON THE SACRED PROMONTORY, NOT EVEN A HEN.

The most valuable diamonds are coloured blue-white.

THE ROMANS DIDN'T USE CATS TO CATCH MICE. THEY USED WEASELS INSTEAD.

April

Benjamin Franklin, the American statesman who played such an important part in his country's early years of independence, died on 17 April 1790. He had been the youngest son of a youngest son of a youngest son of a youngest son.

Franklin once gave an all electric picnic at which a turkey, that had been killed by an electric shock, was cooked over a primitive form of electric stove while being turned on an electrically operated spit.

THE ANCIENT CHINESE BELIEVED THAT SPERM CAME FROM THE BRAIN.

According to experts of haute cuisine the only part of a reindeer worth eating is its tongue, and even that should be smoked first.

18

An earthquake struck the west-coast city of San Francisco on the morning of 18 April 1906. As the city authorities fought to put out the fires that raged after the shockwaves, the Italian tenor, Enrico Caruso, dashed about the city singing at the top of his voice, grasping a picture of the president as he serenaded the destruction.

The atomic scientist, Albert Einstein, died on 18 April 1955. Before evolving his revolutionary theory of relativity, Einstein had worked as a clerk in a patents office.

IN MANY PLACES IN SIBERIA MILK IS SOLD IN THE FORM OF A GIANT ICE-LOLLY, FROZEN ON A STICK.

April

19 Grace Kelly married Prince Rainier of Monaco on 19 April 1956. She became the first film star to appear on a postage stamp, when the stamp commemorating their wedding was released.

The famous politician Benjamin Disraeli, died on 19 April 1881. Among his many achievements as a statesman, he was the first Prime Minister to return to England from Germany bringing 'peace with honour'.

OVER THE YEARS THERE HAVE BEEN MANY ATTEMPTS TO FORGE THE FAMOUS BASS TRADE MARK. TODAY THE BREWING FIRM HAS EXAMPLES OF MORE THAN 2,000 OF THESE FORGERIES.

The great romantic poet, Lord Byron, died in Greece on 19 April 1824. Although it is commonly known that Byron had a clubfoot, scholars have become rather confused over the years, to the extent that today no one is really sure which foot was disfigured.

THE OPPOSITE SIDES OF A CUBED DIE ALWAYS ADD UP TO SEVEN.

The Dead Sea is more than six times as salty as the Atlantic Ocean.

 **20** Captain Cook made an important discovery in Australia on 20 April 1770, when he caught sight of New South Wales for the first time. Both bees and rabbits were later introduced into Australia from Britain. One became an important source of food, the other became a serious pest.

Adolf Hitler was born on 20 April 1889. Between 1933 and 1945 he was paid a royalty for every postage stamp printed in Germany, because they all bore his photograph.

IN MOST OF THE WORLD'S LANGUAGES THE WORD FOR MOTHER BEGINS WITH AN 'M' SOUND.

April

21 Queen Elizabeth II was born on 21 April 1926. On the day of her coronation she wore no fewer than three crowns.

21 April 753 BC is the traditional date for the founding of Rome. Altogether there are eight cities in the U.S.A. named Rome.

THE PONTE ROTTO, THE FIRST BRIDGE OVER THE RIVER TIBER IN ROME, WAS IN CONSTANT USE FOR 1,717 YEARS.

Apes and guinea pigs are the only mammals, apart from man, that are capable of producing vitamin C in their bodies.

THE EARTH IS FIVE AND A HALF TIMES DENSER THAN WATER.

The word 'cigar' comes from the Mayan word for smoking 'sik'ar'.

22 Isabella, Queen of Castile and Leon, was born on 22 April 1451. It was she who encouraged Columbus to undertake his epic voyage to the New World. However, her sponsorship in terms of hard cash amounted to the same sum that she spent on a couple of dinner parties.

On 22 April 1500, Brazil was discovered by Pedro Alvarez Cabral. A butterfly found in Brazil has the colour and smell of chocolate.

THE FIRST AND LAST LETTERS OF THE NAMES OF THE CONTINENTS ARE THE SAME.

In the Middle Ages women had to go around with their ears covered since these were believed to be erogenous zones.

YEHUDI MENUHIN WAS BORN ON 22 APRIL 1916. ONLY EIGHT YEARS LATER, HE GAVE HIS FIRST PUBLIC CONCERT.

April

23 Today is St. George's Day, and traditionally Shakespeare's birthday (1564). It also marks his death (22 April 1616) and coincidentally the death of the great Spanish writer, Miguel de Cervantes.

Shakespeare is the only English playwright to have written a scene entirely in French in a play with a text otherwise totally in English. The scene is Henry V *Act III Scene 4.*

SHAKESPEARE SPELT HIS OWN SURNAME ELEVEN DIFFERENT WAYS.

America is only mentioned once by name in all of Shakespeare's work. This single reference occurs in The Comedy of Errors *Act III Scene 2.*

SHAKESPEARE NEVER SAW AN ACTRESS IN HIS LIFE. IN HIS DAY ALL THE FEMALE PARTS WERE PLAYED BY BOYS OR YOUNG MEN.

24 The Library of Congress was established in Washington D.C. on 24 April 1800. Today it is the largest library in the world with 350 miles of shelving and nearly 76,000,000 items in its collection.

The novelist Anthony Trollope was born on 24 April 1815. Throughout his life he worked for the Post Office, writing before breakfast and riding an average of nearly fifty miles every day.

THE HUMAN BODY CONTAINS ENOUGH PHOSPHORUS TO MAKE THE HEADS OF 2,000 MATCHES.

The Marseillaise, *the anthem of the French revolution, was composed on the night of 24 April 1791, by Claude Rouget de Lisle. He did not compose it in the port of Marseille though. The famous anthem was actually written near Strasbourg.*

THE AVERAGE SIZED MAN WEIGHS ABOUT FORTY TIMES AS MUCH AS HIS BRAIN.

April

25

The first guillotine was used in Paris on 25 April 1792. The device was named after Dr Joseph Guillotin, who did not invent it, but merely suggested it as a humane method of execution.

Oliver Cromwell was born on 25 April 1599. In actual fact he wasn't christened Cromwell at all. He came into the world as Oliver Williams. His father changed the family name after Oliver's birth.

IN THE BASQUE LANGUAGE THE WORD FOR 'GOD' IS 'JINGO'.

When the Domesday Book was compiled in 1086, it showed that there were 5,264 water mills in England.

THERE ARE MORE BACTERIA IN THE HUMAN MOUTH THAN IN ANY OTHER ORIFICE IN THE BODY.

26

Queen Elizabeth The Queen Mother was married to the later King George VI on 26 April 1923. Their wedding in Westminster Abbey was the first royal wedding in that church since 1383.

Marie de Medici, Queen of France, was born on 26 April 1573. Among her many treasures she owned a dress encrusted with jewels, which at today's prices was worth £6,000,000. She wore it once.

THE ONLY PROVEN WAY OF RETARDING HAIR LOSS IS CASTRATION.

The density of the planet Saturn is so low that if it fell into an enormous sea, it would float.

April

27 The famous Portuguese explorer, Ferdinand Magellon, died on 27 April 1521. However, he was not making his celebrated round-the-world voyage on behalf of his own country. He was sailing under the flag of Portugal's chief rival, Spain.

Samuel Morse, the inventor of the morse code was born on 27 April 1791. Morse in fact made his living from painting portraits and when he set about inventing a code for the electrical telegraph he didn't know the first thing about electricity.

WEATHER VANES FACE IN THE OPPOSITE DIRECTION TO THAT FROM WHICH THE WIND IS BLOWING.

The first law against lynching that was passed in the U.S.A. carried a maximum penalty of four years in prison for anyone found guilty under it.

HORSES DO NOT HAVE COLLAR BONES.

○○○○○○○○○○○○○○○○○○○○○○○○○○○○○

28 Sovereignty was returned to Japan by the Allies after the Second World War on 28 April 1952. In 1933 one of Japan's leading generals died. He was buried with full military honours as was his moustache, which measured twenty inches, and which was buried in a separate casket.

Benito Mussolini was shot dead by partisans on 28 April 1945. In his youth, he had twice been expelled from school for attacking his school-fellows with a knife.

THE FIRST SHRAPNEL SHELLS WERE USED IN THE NAPOLEONIC WARS BY WELLINGTON'S FORCES.

The last witch to be burned in Europe went to the stake in Switzerland in 1782.

ONE ORANGE TREE IN FRANCE LIVED AND BORE FRUIT FOR 470 YEARS.

April

29

Emperor Hirohito of Japan was born on 29 April 1901. Today he is one of his country's leading authorities on the study of fish.

Until the end of the Second World War, Emperor Hirohito possessed divine powers in the eyes of his subjects. Only after Japan's defeat in 1945 did he renounce these in favour of a civilian government.

TWO OF ENGLAND'S MOST POPULAR TWENTIETH CENTURY CONDUCTORS WERE BORN TODAY, THOUGH IN DIFFERENT YEARS. IN 1879 SIR THOMAS BEECHAM WAS BORN, WHILE IN 1895 HIS LIFETIME RIVAL, SIR MALCOLM SARGENT, WAS BORN.

The only connection between Cleopatra's needle, that stands on the embankment in London, and the Egyptian queen, is the name Cleopatra. The monument was standing in Egypt for 1,400 years before Cleopatra was born.

THE BALTIC IS THE LEAST SALTY SEA IN THE WORLD.

30

George Washington was sworn in as the first president of the U.S.A. on 30 April 1789. In his youth he had been a champion wrestler and long jumper.

The state of Louisiana was admitted into the Union on 30 April 1812, exactly nine years to the day after the U.S. government had made the famous Louisiana Purchase from France. The hundred million odd acres of the south and midwest of the U.S.A. had originally been offered to the English government, but they had turned it down. So Napoleon sold it to the American government for about four cents an acre.

EVERY THIRTY FEET YOU DESCEND IN THE SEA THE PRESSURE INCREASES BY ONE ATMOSPHERE.

In the space of eight years at the beginning of the eighteenth century over 2,000 French aristocrats died in duels.

May

1

The seventeenth century poet and playwright, John Dryden, died on 1 May 1700. His brother-in-law was a playwright of sorts too. He was one of the many who tried their hand at improving Shakespeare's plays. In his version of *Romeo and Juliet,* **for example, the star-crossed lovers manage to meet in the Capulet tomb and live happily ever after.**

On 1 May 1865 Paraguay's neighbours, Argentina, Brazil and Uruguay formed an alliance against Paraguay. At the end of the six-year war (1864-70) the population of Paraguay had fallen by 1,180,000 to 220,000, and of these only 30,000 were adult men.

THE FIRST HAIR SPRINGS IN WATCHES WERE PIGS' HAIRS.

On 1 May 1876, Queen Victoria was proclaimed Empress of India. The queen never allowed the royal train to travel at more than 30 mph, and when she learned that it had once touched 40 mph she had the driver whipped and dismissed.

OIL AND WATER WILL MIX, PROVIDED A LITTLE SOAP IS ADDED.

In 1882 in France you could buy a camera shaped like a pistol.

JUST ONE GRAM OF VENOM FROM A KING COBRA IS ENOUGH TO KILL 150 PEOPLE.

May

Leonardo da Vinci died on 2 May 1519. He left behind many of the world's most admired works of art, none more so than the *Mona Lisa*, the world's most famous painting. The masterpiece caused the artist some difficulty however. X-rays have revealed that there are three totally different versions of the same painting behind the one that we know today.

When the Mona Lisa *was missing between 1911 and 1913, having been stolen, six Americans each paid £150,000 for what they thought was the real thing.*

THE *MONA LISA* HAS NO EYEBROWS. FLORENTINE FASHION OF THE PERIOD DICTATED THAT THEY SHOULD BE SHAVED OFF.

The Italian employee at the Louvre, who stole the Mona Lisa *in 1911, was only sent to prison for one year fifteen days. At his trial he had convinced the court that his actions had only been prompted by a patriotic desire to return the picture to the country of its origin, which happened to be his homeland and the country in which he was tried.*

THE *MONA LISA* WAS FIRST BOUGHT BY FRANCIS I OF FRANCE. HE KEPT IT IN HIS BATHROOM.

3

The constitution of Poland was reformed on 3 May 1791. During the Second World War over 22 per cent of the Polish population died.

New Zealand was formally proclaimed a British colony on 3 May 1841. The Tongariro Crater Lake in New Zealand is 6,500 feet above sea-level.

EIGHTY PER CENT OF THE ROSE SPECIES ON EARTH COME FROM ASIA.

One cure for epilepsy that was tried for a while in ancient Rome was the drinking of fresh gladiator blood.

May

4

The General Strike began in Britain on 4 May 1926. But industrial disputes took place long before that. In 1160 BC the builders constructing the tomb of the Egyptian pharaoh, Rameses III, went on strike to demand higher wages.

Ancient Hebrews were prohibited from eating camel meat, but the Egyptians and Persians thought that it was a great delicacy.

A LUMP OF IRON WEIGHING AN ESTIMATED 40,000 TONS FELL OUT OF THE SKY OVER SIBERIA IN 1908.

The famous Spanish matador, El Cordobes, was born on 4 May 1936. With the style and following of a football, or tennis star, Cordobes earned three million pounds in his first nine years in the bullring.

THE DERBY WAS FIRST RUN ON 4 MAY 1780. HOWEVER, THE FIRST PERMANENT ENGLISH RACECOURSE WAS ESTABLISHED AT CHESTER IN 1540.

The word 'gas' has no roots in any language. It was invented by J.B. van Helmont to describe the primary element in all bodies and was based on the Greek word 'chaos' which means 'unformed.'

British troops invaded Madagascar on 5 May 1942. A former sovereign of Madagascar, Queen Ranavalona, prevented her subjects, on pain of death, from appearing in her dreams.

The silk from spiders' webs found in Madagascar is woven into a cloth.

THE GREAT DWARF LEMUR THAT IS FOUND IN MADAGASCAR ALWAYS GIVES BIRTH TO TRIPLETS.

It was only after the disappearance of corsets and stays, following the First World War, that dieting switched from being an exclusively male preserve to a unisex one.

69

May

6

On 6 May 1536, King Henry VIII ordered the Bible to be placed in every church in England. According to one count, the Bible contains 66 books, 1189 chapters, 33,173 verses, 773,692 words and 3,586,489 letters.

In spite of this staggering total though, there are still more acres in Yorkshire than words in the Bible.

IN THE BIBLE THE NINETEENTH CHAPTER OF THE SECOND BOOK OF KINGS AND THE THIRTY-SEVENTH CHAPTER OF ISAIAH ARE ALMOST IDENTICAL.

The word 'girl' occurs only once in the Bible.

ONE COUNT SHOWED THAT THE WORD 'AND' OCCURS 46,227 TIMES IN THE BIBLE.

7

On 7 May 1840, Peter Ilyich Tchaikovsky was born. For over a dozen years during his turbulent life he was supported by a wealthy female admirer, who funded him on the condition that they never met each other.

The French novelist, Gustave Flaubert, died on 7 May 1880. His best-remembered novel, Madame Bovary, sent shockwaves through French society when it was published in 1856. It was censured as being pornographic and was charged with offending religion and public morality. But the French public didn't seem to mind. While the novel was being hauled over the coals in court, it was selling by the thousands outside.

CHICAGO AND MADRID LIE ALMOST DUE WEST OF ROME.

There is no reference to a duck anywhere in the Old Testament.

May

8

The German armed forces unconditionally surrendered on 8 May 1945, ending the war in Europe. The Second World War was the costliest in human lives ever fought. The total number of fatalities among civilians and those in active service is reckoned to have been 54,800,000 — a total that is greater than the present day population of Great Britain.

The former U.S. president, Harry S. Truman, was born on 8 May 1884. His middle initial 'S' doesn't actually stand for anything. Because both his grandfathers had names that began with an 'S', Truman's parents gave their son the initial, but to avoid favouritism didn't give a name to go with it.

EARLY IN HER REIGN QUEEN ELIZABETH I SIGNED AN ACT THAT PASSED A TAX ON ALL WHO WORE WHISKERS.

9

On 9 May 1671, Colonel Thomas Blood tried to steal the Crown Jewels from the Tower of London. Yet instead of being executed when he was caught, the thief was rewarded by the king, Charles II. He gave him estates in Ireland and an annual sum of £500 a year.

There are over 400 jewels in the St. Edward's crown that is used to crown British monarchs.

IN AN EFFORT TO CONTROL THE EXPANDING LION POPULATION IN GREAT BRITAIN, LIONESSES AT A NUMBER OF ZOOS HAVE BEEN PUT ON THE PILL.

Water accounts for two thirds of our body weight.

DECIMAL CURRENCY WAS ADOPTED BY GREAT BRITAIN IN 1971, WHICH PUT A HEAVY STRAIN ON THE ROYAL MINT. THEY WEREN'T ALWAYS WORKED OFF THEIR FEET THOUGH. IN 1933 ONLY FOUR PENNIES WERE PRODUCED.

May

10

The Indian Mutiny broke out on 10 May 1857. During the course of the mutiny many ingenious ways of sending messages through the enemy lines were dreamt up. One of these was to send invisible messages written with a mixture of milk and lemon juice.

By coincidence the mutiny broke out on the anniversary of the start of the impeachment proceedings against a former governor of Bengal, Warren Hastings. On 10 May 1787, Edmund Burke impeached Hastings for his alleged ill-treatment of his Indian subjects.

THE DANCER, FRED ASTAIRE, WAS BORN ON 10 MAY 1899. WHEN HE ROSE TO STARDOM AND SUCCESS HIS LEGS WERE INSURED FOR $650,000.

More hunters have been killed by the Cape Buffalo than by any other wild animal.

11

The state of Minnesota achieved statehood on 11 May 1858. One law in the state prohibits the hanging of male and female underwear on the same washing-line.

The only British Prime Minister ever to be assassinated, Spencer Perceval, was shot dead on 11 May 1812. Thirty-four years earlier to the day another British Prime Minister, William Pitt, Earl of Chatham, died.

A DUTY OF FOUR SHILLINGS WAS LEVIED ON EVERY GALLON OF COFFEE MADE AND SOLD IN ENGLAND IN 1660.

Irving Berlin, the songwriter and composer of 'White Christmas' was born on 11 May 1888. His real name was Israel Baline.

THERE WAS AN OUTBREAK OF THE PLAGUE IN SUSSEX IN 1910.

May

12

Florence Nightingale, the Lady of the Lamp in the Crimea, was born on 12 May 1820. For years she carried a pet owl around in her pocket.

When the city after which Florence Nightingale was named, and in which she was born, was flooded by the River Arno in 1966, an estimated £57,000,000 worth of damage was done to Florentine art treasures.

TURTLES HAVE NO TEETH.

Two nineteenth century French composers, Jules Massenet and Gabriel Fauré were born today. Massenet was born on 12 May 1842 and Fauré was born exactly three years later. Today also marks the death of the Czech composer who founded his country's distinctive musical style, Bedrich Smetana.

THE APPLE IS THE MOST CULTIVATED FRUIT ON EARTH. THE PEAR RANKS SECOND.

◔◔◔◔◔◔◔◔◔◔◔◔◔◔◔◔◔◔◔◔◔◔◔◔◔◔◔◔◔◔◔

13

The first permanent English settlement was established at Jamestown in Virginia on 13 May 1607. In the early days of the colony, conspiring to damage or destroy a tobacco plant was considered such a severe offence that it carried the death penalty.

During the average winter, more snow falls in Virginia than in the Arctic Lowlands.

WHEN WE ARE BORN, OUR MUSCLES HAVE ONLY ONE FORTIETH OF THEIR EVENTUAL STRENGTH AND POWER.

The Presidency of Quito changed its name to the Republic of Ecuador on 13 May 1830. The so-called Panama hat in fact originated in Ecuador. It has nothing to do with Panama, except for sharing its name.

May

14

Israel was proclaimed independent on 14 May 1948. Near Jerusalem there is the Forest of Martyrs that contains six million trees, one for each of the Jews that died in Nazi Europe.

We use eight times as many calories in walking fast as we use when we are writing a letter.

HUMAN BEINGS HAVE EIGHT BONES IN EACH WRIST.

Giraffes show affection for each other by pressing their necks together.

ONE INDIAN POEM CALLED THE *MAHABHARATA* CONTAINS ALMOST THREE MILLION WORDS.

Tests have shown that mothers who smoke produce lighter babies than mothers who do not smoke.

15

The (third) Royal Opera House was opened at Covent Garden on 15 May 1858. Compared with the handful of opera companies in this country, the Germans are far better served. There are some sixty permanent opera companies in Germany today.

The first space-ship launched, Sputnik IV, left the ground on 15 May 1960, on the anniversary of the inauguration of the world's first regular air-mail service.

CARLING BLACK LABEL IS BRITAIN'S BIGGEST SELLING DRAUGHT LAGER.

The first broadcast quiz programme ever made was produced in Canada on 15 May 1935.

May

16

The first Oscars were awarded by the Academy of Motion Picture Arts and Sciences in Hollywood on 16 May 1929. During the Second World War the Oscars that were presented were all made of wood, to conserve valuable stocks of metal.

The Dambusters attacked the great dams of the Ruhr on 16 May 1943. The wall of water they sent hurtling into the industrial heartland of Germany was twenty-five feet high and weighed over three hundred million tons.

DURING SOME TRIALS IN ANCIENT BRITAIN THE SUSPECT WAS MADE TO SWALLOW A SLICE OF BREAD AND CHEESE.

Charles I was crowned King of Scotland in Edinburgh on 16 May 1633. During his reign he inaugurated the Royal Mail, although in those days it was the person who received the letter who had to pay for it.

📖📖📖📖📖📖📖📖📖📖📖📖📖📖📖📖📖📖📖📖📖📖

17

Norway was proclaimed independent on 17 May 1814. Three-quarters of all the people in Norway live within ten miles of the sea.

The sun shines on the island of Spitzbergen, which is part of Norway, for three and a half months without a break during the height of the summer.

MANY HOUSES IN THE NORWEGIAN COUNTRYSIDE HAVE ROOFS MADE OUT OF TURF, WHICH MAKES THEM LOOK AS IF THEY HAVE LAWNS GROWING ON TOP; WHICH IN FACT THEY HAVE.

During the 1930's one enormous ice sheet on Spitzbergen moved twelve miles in three years, which was about the same as the Isle of Wight shifting slightly less than sixty feet every day.

May

18

Napoleon Bonaparte was proclaimed Emperor of France on 18 May 1804. However, when it came to his coronation, he refused to be crowned by the Pope and insisted on crowning himself to indicate his independence from the church.

The last Tsar of Russia, Nicholas II, was born on 18 May 1868. Among the schemes that he seriously considered during his reign were: building a bridge across the Bering Straits and surrounding the whole of Russia with an electric fence.

HERRINGS HAVE THE SAME NUTRITIONAL VALUE AS STEAK.

For hundreds of years artists have been in a quandary over whether or not Adam should be painted with a navel.

19

Today is the feast day of St. Dunstan who crowned Edgar, King of All England, in Bath in 973. The coronation rite that he used on that day has been used in the coronations of English monarchs ever since.

The former Prime Minister of England, William Ewart Gladstone, died on 19 May 1898. Throughout his life he made a point of chewing every mouthful of food thirty-two times.

DUE TO THE SHORTAGE OF TOBACCO IN GERMANY DURING THE GREAT WAR, GERMAN TROOPS WERE ENCOURAGED TO SMOKE THE LEAVES OF BEECH TREES.

Anne Boleyn, Henry VIII's second wife, was executed on 19 May 1536. She spent the night before her execution in the very room in which she had slept the night before she was crowned queen.

IN 1685 THE AVERAGE ENGLISH WORKER WAS EARNING 20P PER WEEK.

May

20 Today marks the death of Christopher Columbus, who died in 1506. The total cost of his expedition to discover America amounted to a little over £3,500 at today's prices.

However, he didn't set foot on the American mainland until his third voyage in 1498, when he stepped ashore in Venezuela at a point now called Crisobal Colon after him. (This was in fact the only way in which he ever signed his name.)

THE FEAR OF CLOTHING IS KNOWN AS VESTIPHOBIA.

A great French novelist, and almost as great gourmand, Honoré de Balzac was born on 20 May 1799. On one occasion he sat down to a splendid meal and didn't get up again until he had eaten 110 oysters, two partridges, a duck, twelve cutlets, a dozen pears and a variety of desserts.

☽☽☽☽☽☽☽☽☽☽☽☽☽☽☽☽☽☽☽☽☽☽☽☽☽☽☽

21 Today is the feast day of Saint Godric, the man who may have been the first known lyric poet in English, and possibly the first to set English works to music.

The German artist, Albrecht Dürer was born on 21 May 1471. In one of his drawings, entitled Melancholy, *he included a magic square in which all the numbers in each column and row add up to 34:*

16	3	2	13
5	10	11	8
9	6	7	12
4	15	14	1

OSTRICHES ARE STRONG SWIMMERS AS WELL AS BEING THE FASTEST BIRDS ON LAND.

The human body contains enough carbon to make the leads for 9,000 pencils.

May

22 The creator of Sherlock Holmes, Sir Arthur Conan Doyle, was born on 22 May 1859. When he wasn't writing detective stories, he worked as an ophthalmologist.

On 22 May 1885 another famous novelist, Victor Hugo, died. When his novel, Les Miserables, was published in 1862, Hugo wrote to the publishers asking how it was going. In reply to his cryptic letter, which consisted of a single question mark, they replied '!'.

WALLPAPER WAS FIRST USED TO DECORATE HOUSES IN ABOUT 1645.

The great operatic composer, Richard Wagner was born on 22 May 1813. He always preferred to compose when he was dressed in historical costumes.

THE EARLIEST FORM OF FOAM RUBBER WAS MADE BY BEATING LATEX IN A FOOD MIXER.

The spider crab found in Japan has legs that can span over ten feet.

23 King Charles II set sail from the Netherlands to return to England after the collapse of the Commonwealth on 23 May 1660. He was the first British monarch to attend a public theatre. He accompanied the King and Queen of Bavaria to a performance of Davenant's opera *The Siege of Rhodes*.

Of all the plants that grow on earth, man only puts about four per cent to use.

THE WATER AT THE BOTTOM OF THE NIAGARA FALLS IS WARMER THAN THE WATER AT THE TOP.

In Tibet and parts of northern India the people drink a type of beer made from rice.

May

24

Queen Victoria was born on 24 May 1819. She was to become Britain's longest reigning monarch, living for four days longer than George III, Britain's longest reigning king.

For forty years after her consort, Prince Albert, had died, Queen Victoria ordered his evening clothes to be laid out each day in Windsor Castle.

DUKE ELLINGTON, THE MASTER JAZZ MUSICIAN, DIED ON 24 MAY 1974. HE WAS BORN THE SON OF A BUTLER AT THE WHITE HOUSE.

The larva of the polyphemus moth eats 86,000 times its own weight.

AN ELEPHANT CAN HOLD TWO GALLONS OF WATER IN ITS TRUNK.

25

Today is Independence Day in Argentina. Argentina is the second largest country in South America and Buenos Aires, the capital, is the largest city in the southern hemisphere.

The smallest horse in the world is bred in Argentina. The Falabella stands only two feet high when it is fully grown. However, it has a tremendous turn of speed and can outrun a racehorse over short distances.

BETWEEN 1925 AND 1927 A SWISS SCHOOLMASTER RODE ON HORSEBACK FROM BUENOS AIRES TO WASHINGTON D.C., COVERING A DISTANCE OF 10,000 MILES.

79

May

26 Napoleon Bonaparte was crowned King of Italy on 26 May 1805. He had conquered the whole of the country by the time he was twenty-six.

British Guiana became the independent Republic of Guyana on 26 May 1966. The town hall and the cathedral in the capital, Georgetown, are two of the largest wooden buildings in the world.

UNTIL THE TIME OF THE CAESARS, ALL ROMANS WERE VEGETARIANS.

Fleas can jump over 200 times their own height.

27 On 27 May 1958, a state of emergency was declared in the island of Sri Lanka. Today Sri Lanka is a world famous producer of tea. But until disease killed off the bushes in the last century, it was a world leader in the production of coffee.

There is a temple in the city of Kandy which contains one of the holiest Buddhist relics, one of Buddha's teeth. This has been preserved in shrines in Sri Lanka for the two and half thousand years since Buddha died, and every year it is paraded through the streets in a jewelled box.

TAMILS IN SRI LANKA CURE THEIR COLDS WITH RED ANTS. THEY TAKE A HANDFUL OF THE ANTS IN THEIR HANDS, CRUSH THEM TOGETHER AND THEN INHALE THE STRONG FUMES PRODUCED.

In spite of its name, the killer whale is classified as a dolphin.

GOAT'S MILK IS MORE WIDELY USED THROUGHOUT THE WORLD THAN COW'S MILK.

May

28 The Duke of Windsor, formerly King Edward VIII, died on 28 May 1972. His family name was chosen by King George V during the First World War. When the Kaiser heard of the change, he demanded that *The Merry Wives of Windsor* **should in future be performed as** *The Merry Wives of Saxe-Coburg.*

Windsor Castle is the largest inhabited castle in the world.

ONE OSTRICH EGG MAKES AN OMELETTE BIG ENOUGH TO FEED TWELVE MEN.

The first tank track was designed by a lieutenant in the Royal Navy.

29 The world's highest mountain, Mount Everest, was climbed for the first time on 29 May 1953. Thirteen of the world's twenty highest mountains are in the Himalayas, the other seven are in the nearby Karakorum Range. If Everest and the other nineteen were laid end to end they would almost stretch across England from London to Gloucester.

A glass cat-fish gets its name because it is possible to look right through it.

THE WATER-PRESSURE IN THE OCEAN DEPTHS IS SO GREAT THAT A BOTTLE DROPPED FROM THE SURFACE WOULD BE BROKEN BY IT BEFORE IT SANK TO THE BOTTOM.

Constantinople (now Istanbul) fell to Turkish invaders on 29 May 1453. Today there are 444 mosques in the city.

KING CHARLES II WAS BORN ON 29 MAY 1630. ON HIS THIRTIETH BIRTHDAY HE RODE IN TRIUMPH THROUGH LONDON HAVING BEEN RESTORED TO THE THRONE.

May

〇〇〇〇〇〇〇〇〇〇〇〇〇〇〇〇〇〇〇〇〇〇〇〇〇〇〇〇

30

The eighteenth century writer and philosopher, Voltaire, died on 30 May 1778. During his life he drank fifty cups of coffee a day.

The seventeenth century Flemish artist, Peter Paul Rubens, died on 30 May 1640. Frequently he wasn't responsible for painting his own paintings. After sketching out his design on a canvas and deciding on his colour scheme, he would turn the painting over to the skilled painters who worked for him in his studio. They would then complete their own speciality in the painting before passing it down the line. At one time Van Dyck worked as part of this 'production line'.

DURING THE YEAR IN WHICH THE BLACK DEATH REACHED ENGLAND, 1348, IT RAINED ALMOST NON-STOP FROM MID-JUNE UNTIL CHRISTMAS.

Dry ice doesn't melt. It evaporates.

〇〇〇〇〇〇〇〇〇〇〇〇〇〇〇〇〇〇〇〇〇〇〇〇〇〇〇〇

31

The Union of South Africa was formed on 31 May 1910. Over half the known species of flowers in the world grow in South Africa.

The Okavango River has more water than all the other rivers in South Africa added together. However, none of the water from the Okavango flows directly into the sea.

SOUTH AFRICA PRODUCES TWO-THIRDS OF THE WORLD'S GOLD. IT MINES THIRTEEN TIMES MORE THAN ANY OTHER COUNTRY.

The Sargasso Sea is entirely surrounded by the Atlantic Ocean and consequently has no shoreline.

IN SUMMER THE AVERAGE TEMPERATURE OF THE RED SEA IS 95°F.

June

1

It's against the law in New York to leave a shop dummy standing naked in a window.

THE MORMON LEADER, BRIGHAM YOUNG, WAS BORN ON THE FIRST DAY OF JUNE 1801. WHEN HE WAS OLDER HE HAD TWENTY-SEVEN WIVES, FOUR OF WHOM HE MARRIED ON THE SAME DAY.

Mehemet Ali became the hereditary Viceroy of Egypt on 1 June 1841. Today 95 per cent of Egypt's population live in the area watered by the River Nile. Yet this only amounts to 3 per cent of the total area of the country. The rest is desert.

A SOLID GLASS BALL WILL BOUNCE HIGHER THAN A SOLID RUBBER BALL OF THE SAME SIZE.

On 1 June 1796, the state of Tennessee achieved statehood. But it wasn't until 1968 that the state legislature abolished its anti-evolution law and accepted the theory of evolution.

ROMAN MEN DIDN'T GO TO THE BARBERS FOR A HAIRCUT, THEY USED TO HAVE IT SINGED.

The first animals with voices were the first four-legged amphibians.

June

2 **Queen Elizabeth II was crowned on 2 June 1953. The St. Edward's Crown with which she was crowned weighs five pounds.**

The huge ruby set in the Imperial State Crown, which is worn by English sovereigns on important state occasions, was worn by Henry V at the battle of Agincourt in 1415 and was presented to the Black Prince by Pedro the Cruel of Castile in 1367.

ROMAN LADIES USED A PASTE MADE FROM VINEGAR AND CHALK AS A DEODORANT.

Today is the feast day of St. Erasmus, who became the patron saint of sailors by virtue of being put to death by having his intestines wound out on a windlass.

IN 1896 WHITCOMB L. JUDSON INVENTED A DEVICE THAT WAS A REVOLUTIONARY WAY OF FASTENING BOOTS AND SHOES. TODAY WE CALL IT A ZIP.

Shoes were fastened with buckles until shoelaces were first used in 1790.

3 **King George V was born on 3 June 1865. During his lifetime he collected 325 albums of stamps.**

On one occasion during his naval career King George V sighted the phantom sailing ship, the Flying Dutchman, while he was sailing in the South Atlantic.

GEORGE V'S ELDEST SON, THE DUKE OF WINDSOR, MARRIED MRS WALLIS SIMPSON ON HIS LATE FATHER'S BIRTHDAY IN 1937.

Babies used to be given honey during their baptism.

HALF THE TOTAL DEAD IN BRITAIN TODAY ARE
CREMATED.

June

4

The notorious profligate and womanizer, Casanova, finally died on 4 June 1798. His death wasn't brought on by over-indulgence however, since for the last thirteen years of his life he lived peacefully working as a librarian in a castle in Bohemia.

Casanova used to boast that he always used British contraceptives, which experience had taught him to be the best. He also maintained that of all the countries he visited, England was the most licentious.

TONGA BECAME INDEPENDENT ON 4 JUNE 1970. THE POLYNESIAN DIVERS OF TONGA USED TO HOLD RATHER UNUSUAL WALKING RACES. THEY COMPETED UNDERWATER.

At one time there were seventy mints in England producing coins, a total which is greater than all the mints in the world today added together.

THE MOST COMMON FIRST NAME IN THE WORLD IS MOHAMMED.

5

The economist, Adam Smith, was born on 5 June 1723. He is one of the three men credited with christening the English as a 'nation of shopkeepers'. The other two were the American statesman, Samuel Adams, and of course Napoleon Bonaparte.

On 5 June 1916 the Arabs rose up in revolt against their Turkish overlords. However, fifty-one years later to the day, Israel launched a blistering attack against her Arab neighbours which knocked out the combined forces of Syria, Jordan and Egypt in only six days.

BABIES CAN BREATHE AND SWALLOW AT THE SAME TIME.

It has been calculated by astronomers that more than 100,000,000 comets revolve around the sun.

June

〰〰〰〰〰〰〰〰〰〰〰〰〰〰〰〰〰〰〰〰〰〰〰〰〰〰〰〰

6

The D-Day landings took place on the coast of Normandy on 6 June 1944. However, in the days leading up to the invasion many of the top-secret code names connected with the assault appeared in crosswords printed in *The Daily Telegraph*. **These included Mulberry, Omaha, Utah and even D-Day itself.**

On 6 June 1599, the Spanish painter, Diego Velasquez, was born. In less than twenty-seven years he was to be the official painter at the court of Philip IV.

MORE THAN HALF THE TIN CANS IN THE WORLD ARE MANUFACTURED AND USED IN THE U.S.A.

〰〰〰〰〰〰〰〰〰〰〰〰〰〰〰〰〰〰〰〰〰〰〰〰〰〰〰〰

7

The dissolution of the union of Norway and Denmark was proclaimed by Norway on 7 June 1905. A pair of Norway rats, that usually produce ten litters of ten young each year, can, in theory, produce 350,000,000 descendants in only three years.

Richard II's queen, Anne of Bohemia, died on 7 June 1394. It is thanks to her that riding side-saddle came into vogue as she developed the technique.

LEMON HAS BEEN SERVED WITH FISH SINCE THE MIDDLE AGES. HOWEVER, THE LEMON WAS ORIGINALLY INTENDED TO DISSOLVE THE BONES THAT WERE INADVERTENTLY SWALLOWED. ONLY LATER WAS IT USED TO AFFECT THE FLAVOUR OF THE FISH.

The jets of water that are used in the manufacture of high carbon steel are so powerful that if one was directed at a floorboard it would blast a hole through it.

ON 7 JUNE 2004, VENUS WILL MAKE ITS NEXT TRANSIT OVER THE SUN.

June

8 The prophet Mohammed died on 8 June 632. At that time the Islamic empire was restricted to a small corner of the Arabian peninsular. Within a hundred years though, the faith had spread to North Africa, Central Asia and India, and in another hundred years time one third of the world had been converted to Islam.

King Carol was restored to the throne of Romania on 8 June 1930. The Carpathian mountains in Romania are still the home of many wild animals that have disappeared in other parts of Europe. There you can find wolves and even brown bears.

EVERY VERSE OF PSALM 136 HAS THE SAME ENDING.

9 The Emperor Nero killed himself on 9 June 68 AD as he was about to be arrested and executed. Although he is traditionally associated with playing the fiddle while Rome burned, the instrument had not been invented by that date and anyway Nero was miles away at the time.

Nero is also the only competitor in the history of the Olympic Games to have been awarded first place in an event without winning it, or without even taking part.

GOLD SOVEREIGNS AND HALF SOVEREIGNS WERE REPLACED BY BANK NOTES IN BRITAIN IN 1914.

The vivid narrator of Victorian life, Charles Dickens, died on 9 June 1870. Throughout his life Dickens always wrote facing north.

THE LONG-TAILED FOWL OF KOCHI, JAPAN, HAVE TAILS THAT ARE OVER TWENTY FEET LONG.

June

10

Lazlo Biro patented his revolutionary new pen on 10 June 1943. During their first full year on sale on the British market 53,000,000 biros were sold, which amounted to nearly one biro for every member of the population.

Prince Philip was born on the island of Corfu on 10 June 1921. He became the first member of the royal family ever to be interviewed live on television when he appeared on Panorama *in 1961.*

11

King Henry VIII married his first wife, Catherine of Aragon, on 11 June 1509. But after he had divorced her and changed the country from Catholicism, Pope Paul III decreed slavery for every Englishman who supported the king.

King George II was proclaimed King of England on 11 June 1727. When he led his troops into battle at Dettingen in 1743 he became the last British monarch to play an active part on the battlefield.

HIPPOPOTAMUS MEAT IS SAID TO TASTE LIKE JUICY PORK OR VEAL.

John Constable, the Suffolk landscape painter, was born on 11 June 1776. Two hundred and two years later however, it was revealed that a dozen major paintings attributed to him were, in fact, painted by his son Lionel.

12

On 12 June 1957, twenty-six stone Paul Anderson of the U.S.A. lifted 2.8 tons, the equivalent of two large cars.

The yo-yo was originally a weapon used in the jungles of the Philippines.

IT USED TO BE COMMONLY BELIEVED THAT EATING CUCUMBERS GAVE YOU CHOLERA.

June

13

Peter the Great of Russia finalised his peace with Turkey on 13 June 1700. Turkey lies on either side of the shortest intercontinental crossing in the world. It is possible to cross from Europe to Asia by driving over a bridge that links the two halves of Istanbul, or by taking the more romantic Bosphorus ferry.

The Boxer Rebellion broke out in China on 13 June 1900. The Boxers were given their name by the Europeans against whom they fought. In actual fact they were all practitioners of Kung-fu, but since there was no way of describing this method of combat, they were simply known as Boxers.

TRANSLATED THE WORD 'KUNG-FU' MEANS 'LEISURE TIME'.

The orchid gets its name from the Greek word for 'testicles'.

THE COMMON HOUSE FLY CAN TRANSMIT THIRTY DIFFERENT DISEASES TO MAN.

14

Today is Flag Day in the U.S.A. and it's also the anniversary of the incorporation of the Hawaiian Islands as U.S. territory.

On the Hawaiian island of Kauai, some areas receive 350 inches of rain in a year.

THE FIRE-CRACKER TREE THAT GROWS IN HAWAII ACTUALLY OPENS WITH A BANG.

The average time difference between one high tide and the next is 12 hours 25 minutes.

THE STARFISH IS THE ONLY FISH THAT CAN TURN ITS STOMACH INSIDE OUT.

June

15

Alcock and Brown completed the first non-stop flight across the Atlantic on 15 June 1919, when they tumbled into a bog in Ireland. On the way over Brown had had to crawl out onto the wings no less than six times to clear away snow that threatened to stop the engine.

The State of Arkansas achieved its statehood on 15 June 1836. One morning in 1974 it rained frozen ducks over the state for ten minutes. The ducks had flown into a belt of bitterly cold air and had been frozen to death by it.

A NEWSPAPER PRINTED IN 1896 QUOTED MR GLADSTONE SPEAKING IN PARLIAMENT ABOUT BEER AS SAYING THAT BASS WAS ONE OF THE BEST DRINKS THAT HAD EVER BEEN PRODUCED SINCE NECTAR WENT OUT OF FASHION.

16

Today marks an important anniversary for everyone campaigning for sexual equality. On 16 June 1930 mixed bathing was first permitted in the Serpentine in Hyde Park.

A twenty-four-year-old English woman pleaded guilty to sixty-one bigamous marriages that she had made in the five years leading up to her trial in 1922.

JOHN CHURCHILL, THE FIRST DUKE OF MARLBOROUGH, DIED ON 16 JUNE 1722. THROUGHOUT HIS LIFE HE HAD BEEN ALLERGIC TO CABBAGE.

June

17 Today was probably the most important day in the life of King John III of Poland. The king was born on 17 June, he was crowned on 17 June, he got married on 17 June and on 17 June 1696 he died.

Iceland was proclaimed an independent Republic on 17 June 1944. The mean annual temperature in the Icelandic capital, Reykjavik, which is just below the Arctic Circle, is higher than that of New York city.

THE ICELANDIC PARLIAMENT, THE ALTHING, WAS ESTABLISHED IN 930 AND HAS BEEN GOVERNING THE COUNTRY CONTINUOUSLY EVER SINCE.

In 1060 a coin shaped like a four-leaf clover was minted in England. The idea behind the coin was that the owner could either use the whole coin or break off the separate pieces one at a time.

THE OLDEST MAN-MADE CONSTRUCTION MATERIALS STILL IN USE ARE BRICKS. BRICKS WERE USED IN EGYPT 7,000 YEARS AGO.

Some cells in the human body are so small that 200,000 of them could fit onto the head of a pin.

18 The battle of Waterloo was fought on 18 June 1815, not in fact at Waterloo but four miles away between two neighbouring villages.

One of the more curious figures at the battle of Waterloo was a travelling button salesman from Birmingham, who found himself in the midst of the fighting and ended up ordering a cavalry regiment to charge, which they did.

THE FRENCH CALLED WATERLOO MONT ST. JEAN WHILE THE OTHER PARTICIPANTS. THE PRUSSIANS, REFERRED TO IT AS BELLE ALLIANCE.

June

⊙⊙⊙⊙⊙⊙⊙⊙⊙⊙⊙⊙⊙⊙⊙⊙⊙⊙⊙⊙⊙⊙⊙⊙⊙⊙

19 The state of Kuwait in the Persian Gulf became independent on 19 June 1961. Today it has one of the fastest growing populations in the world and if it continues to grow at its present rate, it will have doubled in twelve years.

The average income per capita in Kuwait is about the same as that in the U.S.A.

THERE IS NO INCOME TAX IN KUWAIT.

People born in the first three months of the year stand a greater chance of being schizophrenics or manic depressives than those born at other times.

GENERALLY SPEAKING FLIES PREFER TO BREED IN THE CENTRE OF A ROOM.

⊙⊙⊙⊙⊙⊙⊙⊙⊙⊙⊙⊙⊙⊙⊙⊙⊙⊙⊙⊙⊙⊙⊙⊙⊙⊙

20 King William IV died on 20 June 1837. Apart from being William IV of England he had also been William I of Hanover, William II of Ireland and William III of Scotland.

123 British men, women and children died in the Black Hole of Calcutta on 20 June 1756. The term 'black hole' had been applied to the cell in which they were imprisoned long before the notorious event took place. A 'black hole' was a common name for a British military prison.

HENS IN THE U.S.A. LAY NEARLY 1,400,000 EGGS EVERY MINUTE.

A common shrew can eat two-thirds of its body weight every day.

ON 20 JUNE 1863, THE STATE OF WEST VIRGINIA ACHIEVED ITS STATEHOOD. THE STATE OF VIRGINIA IS IN FACT FURTHER WEST THAN WEST VIRGINIA AT ONE POINT.

June

21 King Edward III died on 21 June 1377. During his reign a law was passed that made it illegal for anyone in England to eat more than two meals a day.

King Edward III's battle sword was so huge that it required two ordinary men to lift it.

ONE GALLON OF PURE WATER WEIGHS TEN POUNDS.

Today is the summer Solstice, the day on which the druids gather at Stonehenge to watch the sun rise above the Heelstone. According to Diodorus of Sicily, the moon-god visits Stonehenge once every nineteen years.

THE LIFEBOAT WAS DESIGNED BY A MAN WHO HAD SPENT ALL HIS LIFE LIVING INLAND AND WHO HAD NO PERSONAL EXPERIENCE OF SHIPWRECKS.

22 The Quebec Act received the Royal Assent on 22 June 1774. A later law proclaimed in the Canadian province makes it illegal to sell anti-freeze to Indians.

On 22 June 1817, Windham Sadler crossed the St. George's Channel by balloon. In May 1961 the highest manned balloon-flight reached an altitude of twenty-one and a half miles.

SUNLIGHT NEVER PENETRATES MORE THAN 1,200 FEET INTO THE SEA.

During a severe drought in South Africa in 1973 one enterprising dairy farmer fed his herd with old newspapers and cardboard boxes.

FRUSTRATED AND DISILLUSIONED THAT HIS EXHIBITION WAS SO POORLY ATTENDED THE PAINTER OF HUGE LANDSCAPES, BENJAMIN ROBERT HAYDON, CUT HIS THROAT AND BLEW OUT HIS BRAINS IN FRONT OF HIS OWN WORK ON 22 JUNE 1846.

June

23 Today is National Day in Luxembourg, the country with the most enviable strike record in the world. The one strike that did take place was held in 1942 against the Germans who were occupying the country.

The navigator and explorer, Henry Hudson, was cast adrift on 23 June 1611. The bay that bears his name today is the largest bay in the world, measured by shoreline.

QUEEN BEES MAY LAY AS MANY AS 3,000 EGGS IN ONE DAY.

The nail on the middle finger of the human hand grows faster than any other. The thumb nail is the one that grows slowest.

24 The infamous Lucrezia Borgia died on 24 June 1519. In her early life, she had been married four times before she was twenty-two.

The battle of Solferino was fought in northern Italy on 24 June 1859. The fighting was so vicious that the casualties fell at the rate of eighty-eight a minute for fifteen frightful hours.

THE NORTH AMERICAN TARANTULA SPIDER HAS A STING WHICH IS AS HARMFUL AS A PINPRICK.

The mackerel and the tuna belong to the same family.

A CHAMELEON'S TONGUE IS SEVERAL INCHES LONGER THAN ITS BODY. IT SHOOTS IT OUT TO CATCH THE INSECTS ON WHICH IT FEEDS.

June

25 General Custer made his last stand at Little Bighorn on 25 June 1876. However, Sitting Bull, who is usually credited with the victory, was only a medicine man who stayed behind in camp while the other chiefs, Crazy Horse and Gall, rode out to battle.

George Custer was the youngest man ever to be promoted to the rank of General in the U.S. Army. He was made a General when he was only twenty-three.

FLAMINGOES ARE NOT BORN PINK. THEY GET THEIR COLOUR FROM THE FOOD THEY EAT WHICH TURNS PINK DURING THEIR DIGESTIVE PROCESS.

26 King George IV died on 26 June 1830. The official cause of his death was stated as being: rupture of the stomach blood vessels, alcoholic cirrhosis, gout, nephritis and dropsy.

During his youth, as Prince Regent, George IV attempted to maintain his pale, elegant appearance by frequent blood lettings.

AT AN EVEN YOUNGER AGE, GEORGE IV WAS CREATED EARL OF CHESTER, WHEN HE WAS ONLY SEVEN DAYS OLD.

Between 1849 and 1957 parents who gave birth to triplets were given a royal payment of three pounds.

MIGUEL DE CERVANTES, AUTHOR OF *DON QUIXOTE*, LOST HIS LEFT ARM, WHEN HE WAS 24, AT THE BATTLE OF LEPANTO IN 1571.

The glow-worm is the most efficient form of light production discovered so far.

June

27 Bonnie Prince Charlie made his escape to the Isle of Skye, just as in the song, only in reality he escaped disguised in women's clothing, on 27 June 1746.

THE HUMMINGBIRD CAN'T USE ITS FEET FOR WALKING. IT CAN ONLY USE THEM AS A PERCH WHEN IT WANTS A REST FROM FLYING.

On 27 June 1880, Helen Keller was born. Nineteen months later, illness deprived her of sight, hearing and speech. However, by the age of twenty-four she was a world famous scholar.

THE TARANTULA IS ONE OF THE FEW SPIDERS THAT CANNOT SPIN A WEB.

Today is the feast day of St. Ladïslas (Ladïslas I) King of Hungary. Between 1848 and 1956 Hungary was defeated in the five wars and uprisings that she undertook.

THE ODDS AGAINST A MOTHER GIVING BIRTH TO TRIPLETS ARE ABOUT 600,000 to 1.

28 King Henry VIII was born on 28 June 1491. During his reign it was still possible for a man to be hanged in London for eating meat on a Friday.

Doctors treating Henry VIII for syphilis were convinced that the king had contracted the disease when Cardinal Wolsey inadvertently whispered in his ear.

AS A YOUNG MAN HENRY VIII WAS A CHAMPION HAMMER THROWER.

More than 70 per cent of the earth's surface is covered by sea.

TWENTY PER CENT OF THE CHRISTMAS CARDS SOLD TODAY ARE SOLD IN AID OF CHARITIES.

June

29 The builder of the Panama Canal, George Washington Goethals, was born on 29 June 1858. The Panama Canal is the one place on earth where you can see the sun rise over the Pacific and set over the Atlantic. Goethals cut the canal through a bend in the isthmus which produces this curious effect.

The former U.S. Secretary of State, William Jennings Bryan, was so excited at the opening of the Panama Canal that he even sent an invitation to the Swiss government asking if their navy would like to send a delegation to the opening ceremonies.

AS LONG AGO AS 2100 BC MORTGAGES WERE BEING PROVIDED BY BANKS IN ANCIENT BABYLON.

The great Polish pianist, Ignaz Jan Paderewski, who headed the Polish government twice during his life, died on 29 June 1941. He led the government in 1919 and also led the Polish government in exile at the start of the Second World War.

NO MATTER WHAT A HINDU DOES IN HIS LIFE, HE CANNOT BE EXCOMMUNICATED FROM HIS RELIGION.

30 Zaire became independent on 30 June 1960. Zaire mines much of the world's uranium.

In the central forests of Zaire lives the okapi, the only living relative of the giraffe which was only discovered sixty years ago. The okapi has remained virtually unchanged for 30,000,000 years.

ONLY ABOUT ONE PERSON IN EVERY THOUSAND IN ZAIRE HAS A TELEVISION SET.

Typewriters were originally developed to help the blind.

RATS CAN SURVIVE LONGER WITHOUT WATER THAN CAMELS.

July

1 The artillery barrage that heralded the battle of the Somme was lifted on 1 July 1916 to allow the infantry to make their first advance. During the battle the sound of gunfire could be heard on Hampstead Heath.

LONDON HAS TWICE THE NATIONAL AVERAGE OF ILLEGITIMATE BIRTHS.

Today is Dominion Day in Canada, celebrating the anniversary of the union of the Canadian provinces under the British North America Act of 1 July 1867. The town of Hamilton in the province of Ontario is nearer the Equator than it is to the North Pole.

THERE IS ONE STREET IN CANADA THAT IS OVER 1,100 MILES LONG.

The Canadian River flows nowhere near Canada. It flows through the U.S.A.

PRINCE CHARLES WAS INVESTED AS PRINCE OF WALES AT CAERNARVON CASTLE ON 1 JULY 1969. AT THE AGE OF THREE HE WAS MADE DUKE OF CORNWALL AND BECAME ELIGIBLE TO SIT IN THE HOUSE OF LORDS.

The altitude limit for birds is roughly the same as that for man, the summit of Mount Everest.

July

2

President James Garfield of the U.S.A. was shot on 2 July 1881 (to die on 19 September). Garfield was a gifted scholar; he was even able to write Greek with one hand while writing Latin with the other.

The sixteenth century French astrologer, Nostradamus, died on 2 July 1566. Among his many predictions he anticipated the French Revolution, the rise of Hitler (whom he named fairly accurately) and the destruction of cities from the air.

IN APRIL 1884 THERE WAS AN EARTHQUAKE IN EAST ANGLIA THAT KILLED FOUR PEOPLE.

Of all dogs greyhounds have the best eyesight.

3

Algeria achieved its independence from France on 3 July 1962. In the eastern part of the country some of the sand dunes in the desert are over 1,200 feet high.

The town of Tidikelt in the Algerian desert once had to wait ten years between one shower of rain and the next.

'ROMANCE' ORIGINALLY MEANT 'AFTER THE MANNER OF THE ROMANS'.

Joshua Slocum completed the first solo voyage round the world on 3 July 1898, having left Newport, Rhode Island three years before. He was fifty-four when his epic voyage ended and he had been a sailor all his life, but in all that time he had never learned to swim.

CICADAS SPEND SEVENTEEN YEARS DEVELOPING AS LARVAE, BUT THEY ONLY SURVIVE AS ADULTS FOR FOUR WEEKS.

The first 'blue stockings' were actually men. They were members of literary clubs in London and Paris and could be distinguished by their blue hose.

July

4

Today is Independence Day in the U.S.A. celebrating the anniversary of the Declaration of Independence on 4 July 1776. However, the Declaration of Independence was not signed on 4 July. It was actually signed in Philadelphia four days later.

One American president (Calvin Coolidge) was born on 4 July and three others died today. James Monroe died on 4 July 1831, and Thomas Jefferson and John Adams died at practically the same minute on 4 July 1826.

EARLY CHRISTIANS DID NOT USE ALTARS. THEY WERE INTRODUCED INTO THE RELIGION FROM PAGAN WORSHIP.

Egg yolks are used by forgers of bank notes to make their notes feel like the real thing.

5

Two stalwarts of the British Empire, Cecil Rhodes and Sir Thomas Stamford Raffles, were born today. Rhodes, born on 5 July 1853 founded Rhodesia, while Raffles, born on 5 July 1781, founded Singapore. In fact Raffles also died on his birthday in 1826.

The Cape Verde Islands off the coast of west Africa became independent on 5 July 1975. Though small and remote, the islands do have one very big attraction. They have the second lowest death rate in the months of December and January, in the world.

ON 5 JULY 1865, THE BRITISH GOVERNMENT IMPOSED THE FIRST SPEED LIMIT EVER INTRODUCED IN THE WORLD. THE TOP SPEED ALLOWED IN THE COUNTRYSIDE WAS 4MPH WHILE IN TOWNS IT WAS 2MPH.

Until the nineteenth century, it was common to drink beer at breakfast.

PORRIDGE WAS ORIGINALLY A THICK VEGETABLE SOUP.

July

6

The U.S.S.R. was formally constituted on 6 July 1923. The country is so large that the whole of South America could be fitted inside its frontiers with room to spare.

The American naval hero of the War of Independence, John Paul Jones, was born on 6 July 1747. After his service to his country though, he ended his career commanding the Russian navy of Catherine the Great.

SURPRISINGLY PERHAPS, THE U.S.S.R. IS THE WORLD'S FOURTH LARGEST WINE PRODUCING COUNTRY.

It's possible that the word 'tragedy' may have originated from two Greek words meaning 'goat song'.

KARATE MEANS 'EMPTY HAND'.

7

Hawaii was annexed by the U.S.A. on 7 July 1898. Today the state produces over a third of the world's commercial supply of pineapples.

It is against the law in the Canadian city of Winnipeg to use a bow and arrow in the street.

ONE LAW PASSED DURING THE REIGN OF CHARLES II MADE IT ILLEGAL TO BURY THE DEAD IN ANYTHING BUT WOOLLEN GARMENTS.

Today is the feast day of St. Willibald, who was born in Wessex at the beginning of the eighth century and who died in Germany in 786. St. Willibald was the first known English pilgrim to visit the Holy Land, and his brother Winebald and his sister Walburga were also saints.

KING EDWARD I DIED ON 7 JULY 1307. SEVEN YEARS BEFORE IT WAS CLAIMED THAT HE CURED 1,736 PEOPLE.

July

8 The English poet, Percy Bysshe Shelley, died on 8 July 1822. One of his most distinguishing features was his remarkably small head.

Shelley's wife, Mary, wrote the classic horror story, Frankenstein, which she published in 1818, with an introduction by her husband.

9 Holland was united with France on 9 July 1810. In the Dutch town of Hoorn there is one market that sells nothing but cheese.

Over 2,700,000,000 flowers are grown and sold in the Netherlands every year.

THE WORLD LAND-SPEED RECORD HAS TWICE BEEN BEATEN BY STEAM-POWERED CARS.

Babies are born with about 350 bones. But when they grow older many of these fuse together to leave an adult with 206 bones in his or her body.

SODIUM BURNS FIERCELY WHEN IT IS PLACED IN WATER, YET IT CAN BE STORED QUITE HARMLESSLY IN PARAFFIN.

July

Mongolia was proclaimed an independent state on 10 July 1921. Until fairly recently the most common method of execution in Mongolia was to nail condemned prisoners into wooden boxes and then leave them to die on the steppes.

Mongolia is the largest inland country in the world.

EVEN THOUGH MOST OF MONGOLIA IS PLATEAU, THE AVERAGE HEIGHT ABOVE SEA LEVEL IS ALMOST 500 FEET HIGHER THAN THE HIGHEST POINT IN GREAT BRITAIN.

There are roughly 35,750 more people per square mile in Monaco than there are in Mongolia.

MONGOLIA IS ALSO THE ONLY COUNTRY ON EARTH THAT HAS TRULY WILD HORSES. SO-CALLED WILD HORSES IN OTHER COUNTRIES ARE THE OFFSPRING OF TRAINED HORSES THAT HAVE ESCAPED INTO THE WILD.

11

The sixth president of the U.S.A., John Quincy Adams worked for his country for fifty-five years, starting as a clerk when he was fourteen years old. He was born on 11 July 1735.

Yul Brynner was born on 11 July, 1915. Like many stars he made his way up through showbusiness working in many different fields. In fact he started his career as a trapeze artist.

KILTS WERE WORN IN FRANCE BEFORE THEY WERE WORN IN SCOTLAND.

Today is the feast day of St. Olga, one of the first converts to Christianity in Russia. One of her descendants, Vladimir Monomakh, married King Harold's daughter, Gytha, producing an Anglo-Russian link long before Queen Victoria filled the royal nurseries of Europe.

July

12 Julius Caesar was born on 12 July 100 BC and among his many gifts to posterity he left this month. July has been named after him ever since.

The British occupied the third largest island in the Mediterranean, Cyprus, on 12 July 1878. The island gets its name from the Greek word for copper – kypros – which has been mined there for thousands of years.

THE HUMAN BODY CONTAINS ENOUGH IRON TO MAKE ONE NAIL.

In many parts of Asia the buildings are thatched with rice straw.

13 Buckingham Palace became the official royal residence in London on 13 July 1837, when the first incumbent, Queen Victoria, moved in. Originally Marble Arch had been intended to be its main entrance but it was discovered that the grand arch was too narrow to let the State Coach pass through and as a result the arch had to be moved to Park Lane.

William Wordsworth wrote one of his most famous poems, the lines composed a few miles above Tintern Abbey, on 13 July 1798. Apart from being a poet, however, he was also distributor of stamps for Westmorland.

BOTH WORDSWORTH AND TENNYSON HAD TO BORROW THE SAME SUIT WHEN THEY WENT TO BUCKINGHAM PALACE TO BE INVESTED AS POET LAUREATE. THE OWNER OF THE SUIT WAS SAMUEL ROGERS, WHO NEVER MADE IT AS LAUREATE HIMSELF.

Moist air retains heat better than dry air, which explains why desert nights can be frosty and tropical nights warm.

July

14

Today is Bastille Day in France, celebrating the storming of the hated prison in Paris on 14 July 1789, which started the French Revolution. An anagram of French Revolution is 'violence run forth'.

It has been estimated that the Tour De France that grips the country for three weeks in June and July, costs the French economy over £1,000,000,000 in lost production.

THERE IS ONE VILLAGE IN FRANCE THAT IS CALLED Y.

Every year the French drink the equivalent of 140 bottles of wine for every person living in the country.

15

Today is St. Swithin's Day, which, according to tradition, seals the fate of the English summer. If it rains today it's supposed to rain for the next forty days. However, a survey in the last century showed that in one twenty year period the longest period of rain after 15 July was only thirty-one days, and in that particular year St. Swithin's Day had been dry.

However, the trials and tribulations anticipated by the St. Swithin legend are nothing when compared with the reality of living on Java, in Indonesia, which has an average of 322 days of thunderstorms every year.

NEARLY ONE EIGHTH OF THE EARTH'S SURFACE RECEIVES UNDER 9 INCHES OF RAIN IN A YEAR.

Rain has never fallen on the town of Calama in the Atacama desert in Chile.

DURING ONE TWENTY-FOUR HOUR PERIOD IN 1952, CILAOS ON THE ISLAND OF REUNION IN THE INDIAN OCEAN RECEIVED $73\frac{1}{2}$ INCHES OF RAIN.

July

16 The Norwegian explorer, Roald Amundsen, was born on 16 July 1872. When he set out for his historical Antarctic trip on which he beat Scott to the South Pole, most people thought that he was simply making another voyage to the Arctic.

Nicholas II, the last Tsar of Russia, was killed on 16 July 1918. His reign had not begun any more auspiciously than it ended. A stampede for free presents at his coronation led to the deaths of hundreds of his subjects.

99 PER CENT OF WHAT ENGLISH SPEAKERS SAY, IS ACCOUNTED FOR BY ONLY 2,000 WORDS OF THE LANGUAGE, WHILE 25 PER CENT OF WHAT WE SAY IS SAID WITH ONLY 10 WORDS.

The U.S.A. exploded the first atom bomb in New Mexico on 16 July 1945. Even though the noise could be heard over 200 miles away and the mushroom cloud rose 40,000 feet into the air, the U.S. army put out a bulletin that an arsenal had blown up.

17 Florida was formally ceded to the U.S.A. by Spain on 17 July 1819. Florida is not in fact the most southerly state of the U.S.A. Hawaii is even further south.

The city of Jacksonville, Florida, has the largest city area in the whole of the U.S.A. It is twice as large as the area of Los Angeles.

AS AN ANIMAL-LOVING NATION THE BRITISH SPEND TWICE AS MUCH ON PET FOOD EVERY YEAR AS THEY SPEND ON BABY FOOD.

The diameter of the earth's orbit is almost exactly one thousand times the distance that light travels in one second.

OVER 240 DIFFERENT TYPES OF CHEESE ARE MADE IN FRANCE. EVERY YEAR THE FRENCH EAT NEARLY 40 POUNDS OF CHEESE PER PERSON.

July

18

The legendary Gloucestershire cricketer, William Gilbert Grace, was born on 18 July 1848. During his forty-three year career he scored 54,896 runs, which included 126 centuries and more than 1,000 runs in May.

The great English novelist, Jane Austen, died today in 1817. In her first full-length novel, Northanger Abbey, *she refers to the game of baseball.*

JANE AUSTEN'S NOVEL *PRIDE AND PREJUDICE* WAS ORIGINALLY ENTITLED *FIRST IMPRESSIONS*.

19

Building work started on Liverpool Cathedral on 19 July 1904, and twenty years later to the day, the cathedral was consecrated. The cathedral organ has over 9,700 pipes.

Laos became independent on 19 July 1949. Laos has the widest waterfalls in the world, the Khône Falls, which are over six and half miles wide.

PYRITOLOGY IS THE STUDY AND ANALYSIS OF BLOW PIPES.

Three popular first names chosen for their children by nineteenth century Americans were: Aberdeen, Glasgow and Dublin.

IT IS IMPOSSIBLE TO SNEEZE AND KEEP ONE'S EYES OPEN AT THE SAME TIME.

July

20

Sir Edmund Hillary was born on 20 July 1919. Apart from being one of the first two men to reach the top of the world, when he and Tenzing scaled Mount Everest, he also led the first expedition that crossed the Antarctic continent from one sea to the other.

The yak is a very mixed-up animal. It has the skeleton of a bison, the hair of a goat, the head of a cow, the tail of a horse and it grunts like a pig.

AN ALBATROSS CAN FLY ALL DAY WITHOUT HAVING TO FLAP ITS WINGS ONCE.

One pickpocket deported to Australia for his crimes eventually became chief of police in Parramatta.

ONLY THE COCK NIGHTINGALE SINGS.

21

The celebrated late eighteenth century fat man, Daniel Lambert, died in Stamford, Lincolnshire, on 21 July 1809. Weighing over 50 stone (52 st. 11 lbs) he stood 5 feet 11 inches high and had a girth of 7 feet 8 inches.

The first time in which rings were recorded as being used in wedding ceremonies was during the ancient Egyptian civilization, when in hieroglyphics the circle represented eternity.

ONE ESTIMATE STATES THAT PEOPLE IN NORTH AMERICA ARE CARRYING ROUND OVER 200,000,000 LBS OF SPARE FLESH.

Wire wool burns quicker than sheep's wool.

DURING OUR LIFETIME WE EACH EAT ABOUT THE COMBINED WEIGHT OF SIX LARGE ELEPHANTS.

The common garden spider has about six hundred silk glands, and it can lay up to the same number of eggs at one time.

July

22 The battle of Salamanca was fought on 22 July 1812, which happens also to be the anniversary of the death of one of the youngest European university heads. Gasper De Olivares died on 22 July 1645, having being made head of the University of Salamanca when he was twelve years old.

The Mormons arrived in Salt Lake City on 22 July 1847. During the Depression of the 1930's, less than ninety years later, they refused any federal aid, placing their faith in the Lord for their agricultural and economic survival.

THE IMPERIAL ECONOMIC CONFERENCE BEGAN IN OTTAWA, CANADA, ON 22 JULY 1932. THE CITY HAS A CURIOUS LAW THAT PROHIBITS THE BUZZING OF BEES.

23 Ulysses S. Grant, former soldier and U.S. President, died on 23 July 1885. On one occasion during his term of office as President, he had been arrested and fined $20 for exceeding a Washington speed limit on his horse.

Bears are so strong that some of the largest grizzlys have been known to break the necks of full-grown bison with one mighty blow.

DURING ONE CONTROLLED EXPERIMENT INTO THE LIFE-STYLE OF DRAGONFLIES, ONE DRAGONFLY ATE FORTY HOUSE FLIES IN LESS THAN TWO HOURS.

Today is National Day in Poland. In Poland certain animals are regarded as harbingers of good or evil and their appearance is carefully noted. Crows, wolves and pigeons are believed to bring bad luck, while the goat is taken as a sign of good luck.

THE ANCIENT EGYPTIANS USED TO SLEEP ON PILLOWS OF STONE.

July

24 The author of *The Count of Monte Cristo* and *The Three Musketeers*, **Alexandre Dumas, was born on 24 July 1802.** **At one stage in his life he suffered from terrible insomnia and one doctor suggested a novel cure for him, more from desperation than sound medical experience. He told his patient to eat an apple beneath the Arc de Triomphe every morning at seven o'clock.**

Símon Bolívar, who led the liberation movements in five South American countries was born on 24 July 1783. One of these countries was named Bolivia in his honour, and today its capital, La Paz, is the highest capital in the world. It is three and half times higher than the summit of Snowdon.

SINCE WINNING ITS INDEPENDENCE FROM SPAIN, HOWEVER, BOLIVIA HAS BEEN FAR FROM SETTLED. IN FACT THERE HAVE BEEN OVER 180 REVOLUTIONS IN THE COUNTRY SINCE 1825.

25 The first aeroplane crossing of the English Channel was made on 25 July 1909 by Louis Blériot. Fifty years later another Channel crossing made history when the first hovercraft, *SRN 1*, crossed from Calais to Dover.

The great romantic poet, Samuel Taylor Coleridge, died on 25 July 1834. He wrote his famous unfinished poem, Kubla Khan, directly from a dream. He was getting on with it like a house on fire when a visitor interrupted his flow of ideas and when the visitor had gone, so had the dream.

THE MOST POPULAR HOBBY IN THE WORLD IS STAMP COLLECTING.

July

26

The Republic of Liberia was proclaimed independent on 26 July 1847. Liberia is the oldest independent republic in West Africa and the second oldest negro republic in the world.

Today is the feast day of St. Ann who, according to one apocryphal account, was the mother of the Virgin Mary.

A COW HAS FOUR STOMACHS.

A baby has more copper in its brain and liver than an adult.

BEFORE ELECTRIC CIRCUITS WERE INSTALLED IN CARS, THEY CARRIED SIDE-LIGHTS THAT BURNED OIL.

An owl needs some light in order to see in the dark. It cannot see in total darkness.

THE WORD 'SCHOOL' IS DERIVED FROM THE GREEK WORD WHICH MEANS 'LEISURE'.

Mrs Grace Baner of Oswego, New York, claims to be the world's most successful witch. In 1978 she performed over one thousand spells and, according to her followers, all of them worked.

27

Today is the feast day of St. Pantaleon, a popular saint amongst the medical profession because he too was a doctor. However, one of the saint's relics kept in southern Italy, defies medical explanation. This is a phial of his blood, which in spite of leaving the saint's body early in the fourth century, can still be seen today displaying the phenomenon of liquefaction.

The English poet and historian, Hilaire Belloc, was born on 27 July 1870. He was a keen walker all his life and while he was studying at Oxford he once walked to London, covering the fifty odd miles in just eleven and a half hours.

July

28 Peru declared itself independent from Spain on 28 July 1821. One of the great South American mysteries can be seen from the air over the Peruvian desert. Huge drawings of animals, flowers and gods, carved into the ground between 1,600 and 800 years ago still baffle scientists and anthropologists. Some of the lines are nearly forty miles long, but who drew them and why they were drawn, no one has yet discovered.

The master of eighteenth century organ music, Johann Sebastian Bach, died on 28 July 1750, leaving behind a lineage that produced over a hundred cathedral organists.

DAFFODILS ARE ALSO KNOWN AS LENT LILIES.

The coal that is mined in Great Britain today was formed betwen 270 and 300 million years ago.

29 There was a military coup in Nigeria on 29 July 1975. Only ten years before, the serendipity berry had been found in the country. This berry is 1,500 times sweeter than sugar.

Not all violence in Nigeria stems from politics. On one occasion a witch doctor was sentenced to death for shooting dead one of his patients. Apparently he was trying out a bullet-proof charm at the time.

THE NIGERIAN CAPITAL, LAGOS, IS THE LARGEST ALL-BLACK CITY IN THE WORLD.

The Dutch impressionist painter, Vincent van Gogh, died on 29 July 1890, after shooting himself a couple of days earlier. This marked the end of a turbulent two years in the artist's life, which began when he cut off one of his ears. For all his insanity however, he produced his most famous paintings in this period. During his lifetime though, he is only known to have sold one painting.

DOGS SWEAT THROUGH THEIR PAWS.

July

30

England won the World Cup for the last time on 30 July 1966. England's failure to qualify for the finals in later years can be excused partly by the fact that of the forty-five countries that take part in the World Cup, only one, Brazil, has qualified in all eleven competitions.

The English poet, Thomas Gray, died on 30 July 1771, leaving behind one of the most popular poems in the English language, the Elegy Written in a Country Churchyard. *Gray's popularity made him an obvious candidate for the Poet Laureateship, which he was twice offered and which he twice declined.*

TESTS ON THE MEMORIES OF GOLDFISH HAVE REVEALED THAT THEY REMEMBER THINGS BETTER WHEN THEY ARE IN COLD WATER, THAN WHEN THEY ARE IN WARM WATER.

31

Sir Thomas Malory's popular account of the legend of King Arthur, the *Morte d'Arthur*, was published by William Caxton on 31 July 1485. The author wrote this while serving time in prison on a number of charges which included the attempted assassination of the Duke of Buckingham.

Dr Hawley Harvey Crippen was arrested with his mistress Ethel Le Neve, just before their liner docked in Quebec on 31 July 1910. Crippen's arrest made history since it was the first occasion on which wireless telegraphy had been used for police purposes.

THE AVERAGE MEDIEVAL MAN STOOD ONLY 5 FEET 6 INCHES HIGH AND WEIGHED SLIGHTLY UNDER 9 STONE 6 POUNDS.

The Romans used to worship a god called Robigus, who was the god of mildew.

A NOISE OF 210 DECIBELS HAS THE POWER TO BORE HOLES THROUGH SOLID OBJECTS.

August

Today is the birthday of Shakespeare's heroine, Juliet, as well as being Swiss Independence Day.

Even though Switzerland is a neutral country and never goes to war, military training is still compulsory in the country and the Swiss armed forces can mobilize 350,000 troops in a single day.

THERE IS AN ICE HALL ON THE JUNGFRAU MOUNTAIN IN SWITZERLAND IN WHICH ALL THE FURNITURE, WHICH INCLUDES A STOVE, A PIANO AND TABLES, ARE ALL CARVED OUT OF ICE.

The Red Cross took its name and its flag from the Swiss national flag. The Swiss flag is a white cross on a red background, and the Red Cross, which has its headquarters in Geneva, adopted the flag, but reversed its colours to end up with a red cross on a white background.

SWITZERLAND BOASTS ONE OF THE LOWEST UN-EMPLOYMENT LEVELS IN THE WORLD. AT THE END OF 1973, FOR EXAMPLE, FEWER THAN ONE HUNDRED PEOPLE IN THE COUNTRY WERE REGISTERED AS BEING WITHOUT WORK.

Fireflies shine bright enough to glow through a frog's stomach.

August

2

The Canadian province of British Columbia became a crown colony on 2 August 1858. According to laws in the province you can be put in the public stocks for two hours for buying an ice-cream, or a bag of peanuts.

On exactly the same day, the British government took over the Government of India from the East India Company, that had run the huge country before the Indian mutiny of the previous year. Thirty years later nearly 250 people were killed by hailstones in the northern Indian city of Moradabad.

IF YOU SAIL DUE SOUTH FROM VANCOUVER, BRITISH COLUMBIA, YOU DON'T LAND UNTIL YOU REACH THE CONTINENT OF ANTARCTICA.

The Italians drink more wine per person than the Austrians drink beer.

∞∞∞∞∞∞∞∞∞∞∞∞∞∞∞∞∞∞∞∞∞∞∞∞∞∞∞∞∞

3

Rupert Brooke, the poet whose war poems epitomized the spirit of national pride during the First World War, was born on 3 August 1887. However, Brooke himself never saw active service because he died of sunstroke and a mosquito bite in 1915, in Greece, on his way to fight in the Dardanelles.

The author of best-selling English novels like Lord Jim *and* The Nigger of the Narcissus, *Joseph Conrad, died on 3 August 1924. Conrad had in fact been born in Poland and had been christened, Josef Korzeniowski. Even more amazingly, he could not read or write a word of English until he was nineteen.*

UNTIL THE MIDDLE AGES, MOURNERS IN ENGLAND ALWAYS WORE WHITE, THE COLOUR OF MOURNING IN MOST MOSLEM COUNTRIES.

The verb 'to cleave' has two entirely different meanings. It can either mean 'to hew or cut asunder, to split', or it can mean the exact opposite, 'to stick fast, to adhere'.

August

4

Percy Bysshe Shelley, one of the leading English romantic poets, was born on 4 August 1792. He eloped when he was 19, to marry 16-year-old Harriet Westbrook. Three years later, however, he ran away to the continent with Mary Godwin, though he was considerate enough to ask his wife to join them.

King Sebastian of Portugal was killed in battle on 4 August 1578. Portugal is one of Britain's oldest allies. The two countries have never been to war against each other.

'TIP' IS ACTUALLY AN ABBREVIATION OF THREE WORDS 'TO INSURE PROMPTNESS'.

Even though we think that we may have a poor sense of smell, most of us can distinguish 10,000 different smells.

BEFORE THE TENTH CENTURY NO CITY IN EUROPE HAD A POPULATION GREATER THAN 400,000 PEOPLE.

5

On 5 August 1926, the great escapologist, Harry Houdini spent 1 hour 42 minutes submerged in a sealed metal coffin. When he was brought to the surface again and released apparently none the worse for his experience, it was announced that the coffin contained sufficient air to last him 15 minutes.

Today is the feast day of St. Afra, who had formerly been a prostitute before turning to martyrdom.

WHEN BAKED BEANS FIRST WENT ON SALE THEY WERE SERVED WITH MOLASSES. THE TOMATO SAUCE DIDN'T REPLACE THE MOLASSES UNTIL FIFTY YEARS LATER.

Apart from kangaroos, koalas anteaters and sea horses all have pouches.

August

6

The most popular playwright of Shakespeare's day, Ben Jonson, died on 6 August 1637. When it came to burying him in Westminster Abbey, though, the plot was too small for a customary burial, and the great poet was buried in a sitting position.

One of Ben Jonson's successors as Poet Laureate, Alfred Lord Tennyson, was born on 6 August 1809. His career as a poet started early when he wrote a six thousand word poem at the age of ten.

JAMAICA BECAME INDEPENDENT ON 6 AUGUST 1962. ONE OF THE ISLAND'S EARLIEST GOVERNORS, SIR HENRY MORGAN, HAD ORIGINALLY BEEN A PIRATE.

Jesus Christ has appeared in fewer films than the devil.

MARGARINE TAKES ITS NAME FROM THE GREEK WORD FOR A 'PEARL'.

🌙🌙🌙🌙🌙🌙🌙🌙🌙🌙🌙🌙🌙🌙🌙🌙🌙🌙🌙🌙🌙🌙🌙🌙🌙🌙🌙

7

On 7 August 1858, the city of Ottawa was selected as the Canadian capital. Somewhat earlier in its history, Canada had been rented to the Earl of Stirling by King James I for the sum of one penny a year.

In the province of Saskatchewan it is against the law to drink water in beer parlours.

ONE CANADIAN TATTOO ARTIST HAD 4,831 TATTOOS ON HIS OWN BODY.

The Niagara Falls were first illuminated in 1860 and in 1925 the winter was so cold that they froze over.

THERE IS A SPEED LIMIT OF 10 MPH IMPOSED ON TRICYCLES IN BRITISH COLUMBIA.

All the ants that do the work in ant armies are females.

August

8

The Great Train Robbery took place in the early hours of 8 August 1963. Although many of those who took part have been brought to trial, only one seventh of the stolen £2,500,000 has ever been recovered.

After the German collapse at the end of the Second World War, the modern equivalent of over £90,000,000 of gold, currency and gems was looted by troops on both sides when the central bank was broken into.

BETWEEN 1851 AND 1852 FIFTY-FIVE BOYS UNDER THE AGE OF FOURTEEN WERE SENT TO PRISON FOR STEALING SUMS LESS THAN SIXPENCE.

The earliest record of a murder trial dates from one held in Sumer in 1700 BC.

IT HAS BEEN ESTIMATED THAT THE SUN WEIGHS 330,000 TIMES AS MUCH AS THE EARTH.

9

The frontier between the U.S.A. and Canada was defined on 9 August 1842. It is the longest single frontier in the world.

The only Christians who decorate their grave stones with the Star of David are the Basques.

ENOUGH POTASSIUM COULD BE EXTRACTED FROM THE HUMAN BODY TO EXPLODE A TOY CANNON.

King Edward VII was crowned on 9 August 1902, after the ceremony had been postponed due to an untimely appendicitis operation. The king was the first member of the British royal family to own and drive a motor car.

August

10 On 10 August 1809 the people of Ecuador finally rose up against their Spanish overlords. After freedom had been won, the citizens of Guayquil, decided to erect a statue in memory of their local poet, Jose Olmedo. However, a new statue of the poet was more than they could afford, so by way of compromise, they settled for a second-hand statue of Lord Byron instead.

Today is the feast day of Saint Lawrence, the martyr who tradition has it was put to death by being roasted on a grid-iron. By coincidence, it is also the day on which the St. Lawrence Seaway Project was officially launched in North America, on 10 August 1954.

OFFICIAL FIGURES STATE THAT THERE IS ONE ATTEMPTED SUICIDE EVERY TWENTY MINUTES.

One single drop of water contains one hundred billion billion atoms.

11 The first race meeting at Ascot was held on 11 August 1711. Queen Anne was the first person to suggest that Ascot might be a good site for a racecourse.

Queen Anne was, sadly, less successful in her attempt to leave an heir to the throne. All of her seventeen children died before she did.

THE CENTRAL AFRICAN COUNTRY OF CHAD BECAME INDEPENDENT FROM FRANCE ON 11 AUGUST 1960. ALTHOUGH CHAD COVERS AN AREA AS LARGE AS FRANCE, WEST GERMANY AND SPAIN ADDED TOGE-THER, ITS POPULATION IS SMALLER THAN THAT OF PARIS AND ITS SURROUNDING AREAS.

As one of the world's poorest countries, Chad has an appalling shortage of trained medical staff. At present there are over 40,000 people for every doctor in the country. And the life expectancy for men and women is 37 years and 40 years respectively.

119

August

12

Today is not a good day, if you happen to be a grouse. The 'Glorious Twelfth' marks the start of the grouse shooting season. It also marks the anniversary of the first shot fired by a British soldier in the First World War. The shot was not fired in Europe though, it came from a Ghanain soldier involved in the capture of German Togoland in West Africa.

Given a bingo card with ninety-nine numbers, there are roughly forty-four million ways of making bingo.

THE COMPLETE SKIN COVERING A NORMAL ADULT MEASURES TWENTY SQUARE FEET.

Until 1948 the alcohol level of Royal Navy rum was 79.8 per cent. It then dropped to 46.3 per cent until it was finally abolished in 1970.

13

The writer H.G. Wells died on 13 August 1946. An early master of science fiction writing, Wells lived to see many of his predictions come true. He foresaw the outbreak of the Second World War in 1939, aerial dogfights and air raids, while other predictions that came true after his death include air conditioning, world-wide television broadcasts, video recording and automatically opening doors.

The most famous female shot of all time, Annie Oakley, was born on 13 August 1860. On one occasion, the German Kaiser permitted her to shoot a lighted cigarette out of his mouth.

BAMBOO IS NOT REALLY A TREE. IT IS A WOODY GRASS.

America was discovered by the Vikings almost five hundred years before Columbus sailed across the Atlantic to find the New World.

August

14 Two great newspaper magnates died on either side of the Atlantic on 14 August. In 1922, Lord Harmsworth, founder of the *Daily Mirror* and the *Daily Mail*, and later owner of *The Times* died in England. While twenty-nine years later the American press tycoon, William Randolph Hearst died.

A grim chapter of history came to an end on 14 August 1941, when the last execution took place in the Tower of London. The German spy who went in front of the firing squad had been captured after only a few minutes of landing in Britain, though he may well have given himself away in any case; a German sausage was found among his possessions.

APART FROM THEIR GREAT FOOD VALUE, SOYA BEANS ARE USED IN THE MANUFACTURE OF PAINT, GLUE, EXPLOSIVES AND PLASTICS.

15 India became independent on 15 August 1947. The official name of India is not in fact 'India', it is Bharat.

Nine out of every ten Indian girls are married by the time they reach their twentieth birthdays.

IN PARTS OF NORTHERN INDIA CARROTS ARE MADE INTO A TYPE OF PORRIDGE.

The women of the Toda tribe in southern India are given two sets of clothing in their lifetime. They are given one garment when they are children and the second when they are married.

ON AVERAGE WE EACH LOSE 11 OZ WHILE WE ARE ASLEEP AT NIGHT.

More people are killed by bees every year than are killed by poisonous snakes.

August

16

Today is National Day in the tiny alpine principality of Liechtenstein. Apart from the capital, Vaduz, there are only ten villages in the whole country.

For one forty year period, from 1930 to 1970, the governing party in Liechtenstein remained unchanged.

NO PLACE IN GREAT BRITAIN IS MORE THAN 75 MILES FROM THE SEA.

There has been no army in Liechtenstein since 1868.

AT ONE TIME THE PROPHET MOHAMMED REFERRED TO HIMSELF AS A JEWISH PROPHET.

Officers in the Royal Navy didn't have to wear uniforms until 1748.

17

Indonesia became independent on 17 August 1945. The country contains 167 volcanoes, 77 of which have erupted in recent times.

The famous Indonesian flying snake does not fly like a bird, it flattens its body out like a ribbon and glides from tree to tree.

THE RAFFLESIA PLANT THAT GROWS IN PARTS OF INDONESIA PRODUCES A FLOWER THAT CAN MEASURE ALMOST THREE FEET IN DIAMETER.

The youngest 'ancient monument' in Britain was built during the Second World War.

THE ESTUARY OF THE RIVER OB IN THE U.S.S.R. IS 450 MILES LONG.

There is roughly one rat living in Britain for every human being.

THERE ARE NEARLY THREE TIMES AS MANY SPECIES OF PLANT ON EARTH AS THERE ARE SPECIES OF ANIMAL.

August

18 An important birth took place on 18 August 1587. Virginia Dare was born, to the delight of her parents and their neighbours. She was the first white child of English parentage to be born in America.

The Verdun offensive began on 18 August 1917. Using their enormous gun, nicknamed Big Bertha, the Germans were able to bombard Verdun from a distance of seventy miles. The gun had a barrel one hundred feet long and was capable of firing projectiles that weighed a ton.

ONE OF THE MOST POPULAR SINGERS OF THE TWENTIETH CENTURY, ELVIS PRESLEY, WAS BURIED ON 18 AUGUST 1977. DURING HIS CAREER HE HAD EARNED A RECORD 37 GOLD DISCS.

19 The world's most successful jockey, the American, Willie Shoemaker, was born in Texas on 19 August 1931. In just under thirty-one years (1949-1979) he rode over 7,700 winners and won more than seventy-four and a half million dollars.

Roman senators used to wear purple stripes in their togas to indicate their status.

ORVILLE WRIGHT, THE FIRST MAN TO FLY A HEAVIER-THAN-AIR MACHINE THAT COULD SUSTAIN ITS OWN POWERED FLIGHT, WAS BORN ON 19 AUGUST 1871. UNFORTUNATELY HE ALSO BECAME THE FIRST PILOT TO KILL A PASSENGER.

123

August

○○○○○○○○○○○○○○○○○○○○○○○○○○○○○○○○○○

20 Senegal achieved its independence on 20 August 1960. It is the most westerly country in Africa.

The Cyar fishing boats of Senegal are frequently carved from one solid tree trunk, yet some of the finished boats are often large enough to carry between six and eight men.

THE AUSTRALIAN BUSH TURKEY SOMETIMES BUILDS HUGE PYRAMID-SHAPED NESTS THAT WEIGH AS MUCH AS FIVE TONS.

The German army marched into Brussels on 20 August 1914 and exactly fifty-four years later to the day the Russian army marched into Czechoslovakia and occupied the capital, Prague.

MERCURY, PLATINUM, TUNGSTEN AND URANIUM ALL WEIGH MORE THAN GOLD.

○○○○○○○○○○○○○○○○○○○○○○○○○○○○○○○○○○

21 A real-life, female Dracula died on 21 August 1614. Countess Elizabeth Bathori, the niece of King Stephen of Poland, but originally of Transylvanian descent, took to kidnapping young girls and bathing in their fresh blood to preserve her own beauty. When her gruesome secret was discovered in 1610, she had already disposed of 650 victims and she was walled up in her own room for her final years.

The last state was added to the union of the U.S.A. when Hawaii became the fiftieth on 21 August 1959. Mount Wai-'Ale'Ale on Hawaii Island is one of the wettest places on earth. Rain falls there almost every day of the year and there are scarcely seven days in the year when rain does not fall.

KANGAROOS CANNOT JUMP IF THEIR TAILS ARE OFF THE GROUND.

Plasma is 91 per cent water.

August

22 The BBC began its first regular television service on 22 August 1932. This was broadcast on only 30 lines. The high definition, 405 line service did not come into use until 1936.

King Richard III, who probably bore very little resemblance to Shakespeare's villain in the play of the same name, was killed at the battle of Bosworth on 22 August 1485, and was the last English king to die in battle.

THE FIRST ENGLISH BANK WAS ESTABLISHED BY FRANCIS CHILD IN 1603.

In China, the sign of the cross used to indicate a pawn shop.

FORKS ONLY BECAME GENERALLY USED AT MEALTIMES DURING THE LAST CENTURY.

23 The screen idol of the twenties, Rudolf Valentino died on 23 August 1926. When the news of the tragedy reached the outside world, there were several suicides, fans sent 100,000 telegrams of condolence and a memorial was erected to his memory in Hollywood.

The battle of Mons was fought on 23 August 1914. During the British retreat from the battle many of the troops reported seeing phantom armies of mounted knights and archers helping to hold back the German attack. Others even saw angels, the famous Angels of Mons, fighting a rear-guard action.

A CAMEL HAS NO GALL BLADDER.

After Howard Pinxton had won the 1914 Schneider Trophy race held in Monte Carlo, Jacques Schneider himself invited the victorious pilot to join him in the Monte Carlo Sporting Club to drink his success in the finest champagne. Pinxton thanked him for his invitation, adding, "Mine's a small Bass".

125

August

24 The fearsome Mongol leader, Genghis Khan died on 24 August 1227. After each of his victories Genghis used to have his enemies decapitated and their skulls built into huge gruesome pyramids. However, the skull of the opposing general was reserved for a special fate. It was used as the ball in a game of polo.

According to one account the army of Genghis Khan massacred 1,748,000 people in one hour at Nishapur in north-eastern Iran, in 1221.

THERE WERE NO SPEED LIMITS ON ENGLISH ROADS BETWEEN 1930 AND 1934.

25 The beef rearing country of Uruguay was declared independent on 25 August 1825. There is a law in the country that allows duelling on the condition that both participants are registered blood donors.

Ludwig I, King of Bavaria, was born on 25 August 1786. On the same day, in 1845, Ludwig II of Bavaria was also born. Ludwig II had a mad passion for building romantic, fairy-tale castles, which got him into heavy debt and which eventually forced him to imprison anyone who refused to help him with his building projects.

IVAN THE TERRIBLE, TSAR OF RUSSIA, WAS BORN ON 25 AUGUST 1530. AMONG THE MANY ACTS THAT LED TO HIS NOTORIOUS REPUTATION WAS THE KILLING OF HIS FAVOURITE SON IN A FIT OF ANGER.

A new-born kangaroo is only an inch long.

THE ROYAL NAVY WERE FIRING CANNON-BALLS UNTIL 1837, WHEN THEY WERE EVENTUALLY REPLACED BY SHELLS.

August

26 The first man to fly the Atlantic solo, Charles Lindbergh, died on 26 August 1974. Apart from his flying feats, however, he was one of the first people to develop a process of preserving human tissue outside the body and he was also one of the first to develop a mechanical heart to pump blood to the organs and keep them alive while they were also outside the body.

Julius Caesar made his first invasion of Britain on 26 August 55 BC, the day on which 1,401 years later the British used gunpowder in battle for the first time at Crécy.

AN ELEPHANT HAS 40,000 MUSCLES IN ITS TRUNK, BUT NOT ONE BONE.

27 On 27 August 1883 the island of Krakatoa in Indonesia exploded in a violent volcanic eruption. The noise of the explosion was heard four thousand miles away. Rocks were hurled over thirty miles into the air and the dust from the eruption coloured sunsets all round the world.

On 27 August 1920, Percy Fender hit 113 runs not out for Surrey against Northamptonshire, passing the 100 mark only thirty-five minutes after arriving at the crease, making it the fastest century ever scored.

THE OUTSTANDING AUSTRALIAN CRICKETER, SIR DONALD BRADMAN, WAS BORN ON 27 AUGUST 1907. HIS TOTAL OF TWENTY-NINE CENTURIES IN TEST MATCHES GAVE HIM A BATTING AVERAGE IN TESTS OF 99.94 RUNS.

August

28 The great German poet, Johann Wolfgang von Goethe, was born on 28 August 1749. Poetry wasn't his only occupation though. He was also a foreign minister, a fire chief, an actor, a theatre director, a painter and a scientist. In fact he made an anatomical discovery in 1784 which was important to Darwin's work on evolution in the following century.

The first oil strike in the world was made on 28 August 1859, when oil gushed from a bore-hole in Pennsylvania. As recently as 1964, the U.S.A. was still the largest oil producing country in the world.

THE RUSSIAN WRITER, COUNT LEO TOLSTOY, WAS BORN ON 28 AUGUST 1828. HIS MOST FAMOUS NOVEL *WAR AND PEACE* CONTAINS FIVE HUNDRED CHARACTERS.

Peers may not wear gloves in the House of Lords when the sovereign is present.

29 The Australian city of Melbourne was founded on 29 August 1835. Australia is the only country on earth that fills an entire continent.

If it was possible for a man to jump the same height as a flea, relative to the size of his body, then he would be able to jump right over St. Paul's Cathedral.

THE HUMAN BRAIN BURNS UP ABOUT THE SAME AMOUNT OF POWER AS A 10-WATT ELECTRIC BULB.

Chewing a stick is one of the best ways of cleaning one's teeth.

THERE IS A MOSQUE IN IRAN THAT IS CARVED OUT OF SOLID ROCK AND WHICH WAS A CHRISTIAN CHURCH
UNTIL 1254.

August

30 Pedro the Cruel, King of Castile and Leon, was born on 30 August 1334. He was given the name 'cruel' because of his murder of his own brother. However, he got his just desert when another brother, Henry, finally killed him in single combat eleven years later.

Today is the feast day of St. Rose of Lima, who died there in 1617. She was the first person in either North or South America to be canonized a saint.

BUNGALOWS GET THEIR NAME FROM THE HINDU WORD 'BANGLA' WHICH MEANS 'BELONGING TO BENGAL'.

Ladies at the French court in the fourteenth century used to wear their corsets as outer garments.

POPE BENEDICT IX WAS CREATED POPE WHEN HE WAS TWELVE YEARS OLD.

31 The battle of Malplaquet was fought on 31 August 1709. More British troops were killed in this one-day engagement in the War of the Spanish Succession than died in the ten day battle at El Alamein during the Second World War.

Malaya (Malaysia today) became independent on 31 August 1957. Every year the country produces enough rubber to make tyres for well over 55,000,000 cars.

THE DUCK-BILLED PLATYPUS IS THE ONLY MAMMAL WITH POISONOUS GLANDS.

Trinidad also became independent today, on 31 August 1962. The island was originally called Iere, a name given to it by the first inhabitants, the Carib Indians. Translated Iere means 'the land of the hummingbird.'

September

1

King Louis XIV of France died on 1 September 1715, after reigning for over seventy-two years. He had a stomach twice the size of that of a normal man.

Louis XIV only took three baths in his lifetime, and none of those were taken voluntarily.

AT LOUIS'S COURT ONLY HE AND HIS QUEEN WERE ALLOWED TO SIT IN CHAIRS WITH ARMS.

Our first set of teeth, our milk teeth, has twenty-two teeth, although our permanent adult set has ten more.

OF ALL THE SPECIES OF SHARK THAT ARE FOUND ON EARTH THERE ARE LESS THAN TEN THAT HAVE THE TEETH AND JAWS CAPABLE OF EATING A MAN AND FEWER STILL HAVE THE INCLINATION TO DO SO.

The state of Qatar, in the Persian Gulf, became independent on 1 September 1971. It is one of the few countries in the world with no surface water, except for a few salty lakes and wells. Most of the country's fresh water is made in special buildings that extract salt from the water to make it drinkable.

PEOPLE WHO SMOKE TWENTY HIGH-TAR CIGARETTES EACH DAY INHALE HALF A CUPFUL OF TAR EACH YEAR.

Frederick the Great used to be bled during battles to help calm his nerves.

September

2 The Great Fire of London began on 2 September 1666 and raged for four days. Yet in all that time only six people lost their lives.

IN 1975 AN AMERICAN WAS ARRESTED AFTER TRYING TO DROWN HIS WIFE IN A WATER BED.

The man who revived the Olympic Games, Baron Pierre de Coubertin, died on 2 September 1937. The first recorded Olympic Games took place in 776 BC and consisted of a 200 yard foot race.

WE CAN ONLY RECEIVE SKIN GRAFTS FROM OUR OWN BODIES OR FROM THE BODY OF AN IDENTICAL TWIN.

The former president of the U.S.A., James Garfield, had a curious meeting a couple of days before his assassination. He asked Abraham Lincoln's son to relate his father's assassination at which he had been present. Robert Lincoln did this and two days later he was present when Garfield was shot. (Robert Lincoln was also present when President McKindley was shot, and after that he refused to attend a state occasion).

3 Today was quite an eventful day in the life of England's only dictator, Oliver Cromwell. On 3 September 1650 he won an important victory at Dunbar. On the same day the following year he won another victory at Worcester. And seven years later to the day he died.

Two years after his death, Oliver Cromwell's body was hanged and decapitated.

ON THE DAY THAT THE SECOND WORLD WAR BROKE OUT, 3 SEPTEMBER 1939, AN EXCESS PROFITS TAX CAME INTO FORCE IN BRITAIN.

Ten times more men are colour blind than women.

131

September

September

4

Today is the feast day of St. Marinus, the patron saint of San Marino, the tiny state in the Italian peninsular that is entirely surrounded by Italy. According to legend, St. Marinus fled to the area and hid in a hermit's cell in order to escape a woman who falsely claimed that she was his wife.

San Marino is the third smallest independent country in the world and has one of the shortest national anthems. Its national anthem is only four lines long.

FOUNDED RIGHT AT THE BEGINNING OF THE FOURTH CENTURY BC, SAN MARINO CLAIMS TO BE THE OLDEST STATE IN EUROPE AND THE OLDEST REPUBLIC IN THE WORLD.

If you put sugar into a glass of water and then add an egg, the egg will float.

5

Today is the birthday of Louis XIV of France, the Sun King, who was born on 5 September 1638. He shared one feature with Napoleon Bonaparte at birth, they were both born with teeth.

Louis's great interest in childbirth, brought on by his many amours, led him to become one of the first reformers of obstetrics.

DURING HIS LIFE LOUIS XIV OWNED 413 BEDS.

On one occasion Louis XIV greeted the ambassador from Siam at Versailles dressed in a fur robe, encrusted with jewels, that reputedly cost one sixth of the total construction cost of Versailles itself.

THERE WERE STILL GALLEYS ROWED BY SLAVES IN USE IN THE NAVY DURING LOUIS XIV'S REIGN.

September

6 The Pilgrim Fathers set sail from Plymouth on board the *Mayflower* bound for America on 6 September 1620. After her days of service were over, the *Mayflower* was broken up and some of her timbers were taken to build a barn in Chalfont St. Giles, Buckinghamshire, the village in which John Milton lived during the plague of 1665.

By the turn of the nineteenth century Michael Thomas Bass was trading with nine importers of beer in St. Petersburg, with twenty-five in Danzig, with four in Hanover, four in Hamburg and one in Elsinore (the setting for Hamlet), to mention only a few of his sixty-seven importers on the continent.

IN ANY TERMITE NEST, THERE IS ONLY ONE KING TERMITE AND ONE QUEEN TERMITE. ALL THE MILLIONS OF OTHERS ARE THEIR OFFSPRING.

7 Brazil declared its independence from Portugal on 7 September 1822. As the world's top producer of coffee, Brazil produces twice as much coffee each year as India, the world's top tea producer, produces tea.

Brazil is about the same size as the U.S.A. excluding Alaska and Hawaii, which makes it the largest country in South America. It covers nearly half the land in South America and it has borders with ten of the other twelve countries on the continent.

THE MONUMENT AXIS ROAD IN THE CAPITAL OF BRAZIL, BRASILIA, IS OVER A SIXTH OF A MILE WIDE AND COULD ACCOMODATE 160 CARS DRIVING SIDE BY SIDE.

There is one primitive Indian tribe living in the Mato Grosso ('The Big Forest') in Brazil, that has no system of counting and no numbers in their language.

September

8

Richard the Lionheart was born on 8 September 1157. In all he only visited his kingdom, England, on two occasions, while his queen Berengaria never set foot in the country.

New Amsterdam was captured by the British on 8 September 1664 and was promptly renamed New York. In the native Indian language 'Manhattan' means 'The place of drunkenness'.

IN AUGUST 1972, THE MURDER RATE IN NEW YORK CITY WAS RUNNING AT THIRTEEN A DAY.

Two and a half pounds of grain are used to produce one pound of chicken meat; three pounds of grain are needed to produce one pound of pork; while ten pounds of grain have to be fed to the animal to produce one pound of beef.

IN 1610 THE POPULATION OF THE COLONIES, IN WHAT IS NOW THE U.S.A., TOTALLED 350.

9

William the Conqueror died of injuries received from a saddle pommel, on 9 September 1087. Ironically he had been able to jump into a saddle while clad in full armour when he was a young man.

More people die as a result of falls in the home than from any other household accident.

NO TWO ZEBRAS HAVE THE SAME PATTERN OF STRIPES.

The French statesman, Cardinal Richlieu, was born on 9 September 1583. He came from a fairly peculiar family. His sister thought that her back was made of crystal and his brother was quite convinced that he was God the Father.

September

10 The Portuguese colony of Guinea-Bissau became independent on 10 September 1974. Formerly known as Portuguese Guinea, it was the oldest European colony in Africa, having been first visited by the Portuguese in 1446.

In 1973 there was only one daily newspaper in the country and that was only printed in editions of 6,000 copies; which worked out as one copy for every eighty-five people.

A SHARP COUGH CAN SOMETIMES MOVE AIR INSIDE THE BODY FASTER THAN THE SPEED OF SOUND.

The battle of Lake Erie was fought on 10 September 1813. At one end of the lake are the Niagara Falls which are eroding their base at such a rate that some geologists reckon that they may well have disappeared in less than 25,000 years.

BATS ARE THE ONLY FLYING MAMMALS.

11 On 11 September 1973 the left-wing government in Chile was toppled by a military coup. The potato was introduced to Europe from Chile in about 1530.

At one point the frontier between Chile and Argentina is marked by a huge bronze statue of Christ. This is an even more significant symbol of peace, since it was made from cannon that had been used by both armies against each other.

AMONG ITS ISLAND POSSESSIONS IN THE PACIFIC, CHILE OWNS THE JUAN FERNANDEZ GROUP, ON WHICH IT IS BELIEVED THE ORIGINAL ROBINSON CRUSOE, ALEXANDER SELKIRK, WAS SHIPWRECKED.

According to heraldic terminology, the American flag ought not to be called the Stars and Stripes, it should be called the 'Mullets and Barrulets'.

September

12 Wellington's ally at Waterloo, Gebhard von Blücher, died on 12 September 1819. In spite of his bravery on the battlefield, the Prussian general had lived for many years with the morbid fear that he would give birth to an elephant.

On 12 September 1940 five boys stumbled into a cave in France and found the oldest works of art yet discovered. These are the famous Paleolithic animal paintings in the Lascaux caves in France. They date from 30,000 to 10,000 BC.

13 The temperature climbed to a record 136.4°F in el-Azizia, Libya, on 13 September 1922, which made it the hottest that's ever been recorded.

General James Wolfe fell mortally wounded at his moment of victory at the battle of Quebec, while on the other side his opposite number, the French commander also collapsed mortally wounded. The battle only lasted about a quarter of an hour.

APART FROM HUMANS THE ONLY ANIMAL THAT HAS BEEN TAUGHT TO STAND ON ITS HEAD IS THE ELEPHANT.

14 Russia was proclaimed a republic on 14 September 1917. Lake Baskunchak in the U.S.S.R. is a salt water lake, fed constantly by salt springs to the extent that scientists have estimated that there is enough salt there to meet the world's needs for over one thousand years.

Italy's most celebrated poet, Dante Alighieri, died on 14 September 1321. When he was only nine years old he wrote his first sonnet to Beatrice.

ELEPHANTS HAVE ONE OUNCE OF BRAIN FOR EVERY POUND OF BODY WEIGHT.

September

15 The Bulgarian People's Republic was proclaimed on 15 September 1946. Bulgaria is famous for the production of attar of roses and the rose gardens of central Bulgaria are the largest in the world. It takes 30,000 rose petals to make just one gram of attar.

Jumbo the elephant, the great favourite of Victorian circus goers, was killed by a train in Canada on 15 September 1885, exactly twenty-five years after the railway claimed its first victim.

THE WORD 'POLICE' DIDN'T APPEAR IN ENGLISH UNTIL THE EIGHTEENTH CENTURY. ORIGINALLY IT WAS A FRENCH WORD.

Mortality statistics for Americans aged 1 – 14 show that more of them die from accidents than from disease.

16 On 16 September 1810 the Mexican revolt began against Spain. Today the border between Mexico and its northern neighbour, the U.S.A., is the busiest frontier in the world. Every year over 120,000,000 people cross from one country to the other.

Tomatoes were first imported to Europe from Mexico. Originally they were known as love apples.

THE AVERAGE LEAD PENCIL WILL DRAW A LINE 35 MILES LONG.

The world's largest pyramid is in Mexico. It covers an area of 45 acres and stands 177 feet high.

THE EARLIEST AEROPLANES WERE MODELLED ON BOX-KITES.

There are references in the Canon of Jewish Law, the Talmud, to artificial insemination and oral contraceptives.

137

September

17

Today is Constitution Day in the U.S.A, the anniversary of the signing of the U.S. Constitution on 17 September 1787. Nowadays Americans get an average of 150,000 new laws every year.

Today is the feast day of St. Hildegard, a twelfth century German nun, who was one of the most astonishing women of the Middle Ages. She corresponded with kings, emperors and four popes. She wrote countless religious works. She became a prophetess, claiming the power to foresee future events. And in her spare time she even invented a language.

THERE IS ONLY ROOM FOR TWO PRISONERS IN THE PRISON ON THE ISLAND OF SARK.

18

Pope Gregory XVI was born on 18 September 1765. During his papacy the practice of castrating choristers to sing in the choir was still current. In fact it did not disappear until the papacy of Leo XXIII, less than a century ago.

Greta Garbo, the Swedish film star, famous for the line 'I want to be alone', was born on 18 September 1905. Before becoming a film idol she had worked as a manicurist in a barber's shop in Stockholm.

THE SOLAR YEAR WAS FIRST CALCULATED WITH 365 DAYS BY THE ANCIENT EGYPTIANS.

Chile proclaimed its independence from Spain on 18 September 1810. Lying as it does in an area notorious for earthquakes, Chile has been shaken by a hundred major earthquakes in the last four hundred years.

A SNAIL CAN CRAWL ALONG THE CUTTING EDGE OF A RAZOR BLADE WITHOUT HARMING ITSELF.

September

19

The first beauty contest was held on 19 September 1888 and was won by a black girl.

Today is the feast day of St. Januarius, an Italian bishop who died at the beginning of the fourth century. There is a glass phial of his blood in the cathedral at Naples which has been shown to the public eighteen times a year for the last five centuries and which changes from a dried to a liquid state every time. So far no one has been able to explain this.

TO IMPROVE THEIR APPEARANCE, MANY HINDU WOMEN STAIN THEIR TEETH RED.

At first, white bread was used exclusively in church services.

20

As father Padre Pio was kneeling in prayer on 20 September 1918, he collapsed in a faint, only to find, when he regained consciousness, that he was bleeding from the very points in his body where Christ had been wounded on the cross. These wounds, called stigmata, continued to bleed for the rest of Padre Pio's life, which lasted another forty years.

King Saul is the first person known to have committed suicide by falling on his sword.

THE GREEKS AND THE ROMANS BELIEVED THAT SNEEZING WAS A FAVOURABLE OMEN.

Snails only mate once in their lifetime, however the act can often last twelve hours.

September

21 King Haakon VII of Norway died on 21 September 1957, from complications that arose from falling in a bath.

The Federal Republic of Germany came into being officially on 21 September 1949. Its two-week long festival known as the Oktoberfest, mostly takes place in September.

TODAY WEST GERMANY IS THE WORLD'S SECOND LARGEST CAR-OWNING COUNTRY.

Pythagoras put forward the idea that the world was round about two-and-half-thousand years ago.

SOME QUEEN TERMITES HAVE REMAINED FERTILE FOR FIFTY YEARS.

22 The Saharan state of Mali became independent on 22 September 1960. Its first president, Modibo Keita, had worked originally as the leader of a troupe of dancers.

Centuries before the star known today as Sirius B was discovered by astronomers, the Dogon tribe in Mali were predicting when it would next appear, without the aid of telescopes or computers. The star was an object of Dogon worship and they knew exactly how long it took to go round the larger star, Sirius.

DURING THE FIRST HUNDRED YEARS OF ITS LIFE A EUROPEAN ASH TREE GROWS AT THE RATE OF ONE FOOT EVERY YEAR.

Today is the feast day of St. Phocas, a market-gardener who lived and worked on the southern shore of the Black Sea, but who inexplicably became the patron saint of Black Sea sailors.

September

23 Today is the day of the autumnal equinox, one of the two times in the year when there are equal hours of light and dark. The other occasion is the spring equinox.

ON 23 SEPTEMBER 1745 A LONDON COURT FINED A 'TICKET PORTER' THREE SHILLINGS FOR SWEARING.

The discovery of the planet Neptune by Johann Galle was announced on 23 September 1846. However, further examination of astronomical records showed that the planet had in fact been recorded in 1795, only the astronomers who saw it then thought that it was a normal star and simply made a routine record of their observation.

DEIMOS, ONE OF THE MOONS OF MARS, RISES AND SETS TWICE A DAY.

24 On 24 September 1841, the Sultan of Brunei appointed the first rajah of Sarawak in return for the services that he had received from the new rajah in fighting his enemies. The name of the first rajah was (Sir) James Brooke. He was an English administrator who had sailed to the island to put down piracy. Thanks to him the island became a British colony and eventually part of present day Malaysia.

The second German Zeppelin was shot down over England on 24 September 1916, the very day that the French dropped bombs on the important Krupp Steel Works at Essen, in the Ruhr.

THE PRACTICE OF GIVING AWAY BRIDES AT THEIR WEDDINGS COMES DOWN TO US FROM THE TIME WHEN THIS USED TO BE DONE FOR MONEY.

The so-called hurricane plant is protected from being damaged by high winds by large holes in its leaves.

September

25 King Philip the Handsome of Spain died on 25 September 1506, to the great grief of his wife, who, not wishing to believe that he had left her for ever, kept his body in her bed for the next three years.

Vasco Balboa discovered the Pacific Ocean on 25 September 1513. What he set eyes on was an area of sea that was larger than all the land surfaces on earth added together.

THE MARIANAS TRENCH IN THE PACIFIC IS SO DEEP THAT IF AN OBJECT WERE DROPPED INTO THE WATER OVER IT, IT WOULD TAKE OVER AN HOUR TO SINK TO THE BOTTOM.

More women attempt suicide than men in most countries of the world.

26 Today is Dominion Day in New Zealand, the anniversary of the declaration that made New Zealand a Dominion on 26 September 1907. There are twenty sheep for every human living in the country.

Hundreds of years ago New Zealand was the home of a breed of flightless bird known as the moa. These were related to ostriches, with the smallest moas growing to the size of a turkey and the largest ones reaching a height of nearly eleven and a half feet. However, the native Maoris hunted the moas for food and the large birds were extinct before white men even arrived in New Zealand.

NEW ZEALAND DOES NOT HAVE ANY NATIVE SNAKES. THOSE THAT ARE THERE HAVE ALL BEEN IMPORTED FROM OTHER COUNTRIES.

Steel strips are stronger than a solid piece of steel of the same dimensions.

BUTTERFLIES HAVE TWELVE THOUSAND EYES.

September

 **27** Aimee Semple McPherson died on 27 September 1944 and was buried with a telephone in her coffin. During her life she had been a spiritualist and she hoped to continue her work in the after life.

King Louis XIII of France was born on 27 September 1601. During one stage in his life his health caused such concern that in one month he was bled forty-seven times.

SEEDS OF AN ARCTIC LUPIN THAT WERE ESTIMATED TO BE 10,000 YEARS OLD HAVE BEEN SUCCESSFULLY GERMINATED AND GROWN IN A LABORATORY.

The jellyfish known as the 'Portuguese Man of War' is not one single animal but a colony of lots of little ones.

28  **Gamal Abdul Nasser, the former President of Egypt, died on 28 September 1970. The crowd that attended his funeral in Cairo was one of the largest ever seen in Egypt. An estimated four million people thronged the capital to pay their last respects to their dead leader.**

The great pyramids of Egypt were once even more impressive than they are today. Originally they were covered with marble.

THE SYMBOL FOR A HAPPY MARRIAGE IN ANCIENT GREECE WAS A TRIANGLE.

Poodles do not moult.

ARABIC WAS NOT GENERALLY SPOKEN IN EGYPT UNTIL THE SEVENTEENTH CENTURY.

September

29

England's greatest naval commander, Horatio Lord Nelson, was born on 29 September 1758. Imposing as he was in battle, he was physically unimpressive, being thin and short. He stood a mere 5 feet 4 inches tall.

Robert Clive, the man who established British control in India, was born on 29 September 1725. During his early days in India, he became so depressed that he tried to commit suicide. But on both occasions his pistol failed to fire and he decided that he must be destined to achieve something.

A NUT FOUND IN SOUTH AMERICA THAT EXPLODES WHEN IT IS RIPE IS KNOWN APPROPRIATELY AS THE *MONKEY'S DINNER BELL*.

When astronauts shave in space they have to use razors with a vacuum attachment that sucks in the bristles as they are shaved. Without this the bristles would float about inside the capsule.

@@@@@@@@@@@@@@@@@@@@@@@@@@@@@@@@

30

Jack the Ripper claimed two victims in the early hours on 30 September 1888. Although the identity of the mass murderer was never proved the police did discover one important fact about the man, or woman, they were hunting. Jack was left-handed.

The Munich Agreement was signed on 30 September 1938, yet exactly a year later the British public were being issued with identity cards at the start of the Second World War.

THE SILK WORM MOTH HAS ELEVEN BRAINS.

Screwdrivers were invented before screws. Originally they were used to extract bent nails.

THE ONLY MAMMALS THAT AREN'T COLOUR BLIND ARE MAN AND MONKEYS.

October

1

King Henry III of England was born on 1 October 1207. Only ten years later he inherited the throne.

Today is a national holiday in China commemorating the formation of the Central People's Government on 1 October 1949. The Chinese name for China, zhong guo, means 'the middle kingdom'.

BEFORE THE CHINESE TAKEOVER OF TIBET, ONE IN FOUR OF THE MEN IN THE COUNTRY WERE BUDDHIST MONKS.

You can identify cattle by their nose prints just as you can identify human beings by their finger prints.

POLLUTION IS SO BAD IN THE SARGASSO SEA THAT THERE IS MORE OIL ON THE SURFACE THAN THE SEAWEED THAT GIVES THE SEA ITS NAME.

Left-handed playing cards have pips in all four corners, whereas normal playing cards have them only in the top left-hand corner.

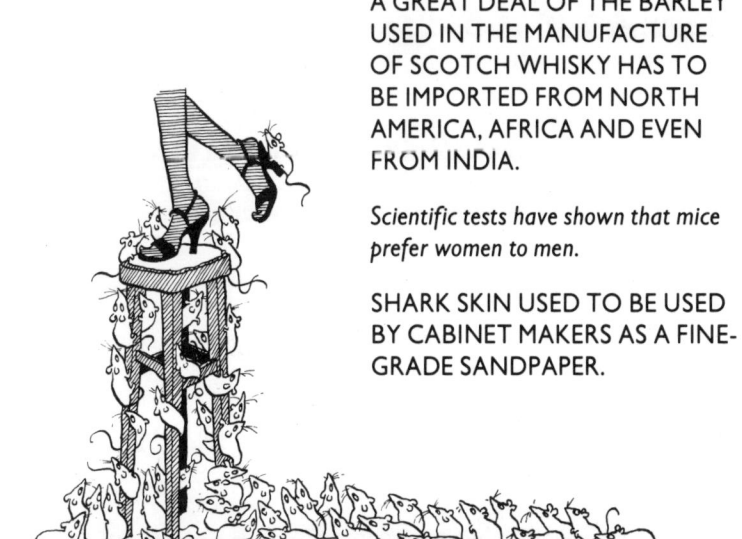

A GREAT DEAL OF THE BARLEY USED IN THE MANUFACTURE OF SCOTCH WHISKY HAS TO BE IMPORTED FROM NORTH AMERICA, AFRICA AND EVEN FROM INDIA.

Scientific tests have shown that mice prefer women to men.

SHARK SKIN USED TO BE USED BY CABINET MAKERS AS A FINE-GRADE SANDPAPER.

October

2

Mahatma Gandhi was born on 2 October 1869. In spite of his strict Hindu upbringing and his later trappings of poverty and simplicity, Gandhi spent several years experiencing life in Britain. When he was asked once what he thought about western civilization he replied that he thought it would be a very good idea.

The first British submarine was launched at Barrow on 2 October 1901. Unless it is sitting on the bottom, a submarine cannot remain stationary. It must move either vertically or horizontally, if it is underwater.

DURING THE FIRST SIX MONTHS OF THE SECOND WORLD WAR, ONE U-BOAT CAPTAIN ALONE SANK FORTY-FIVE ALLIED SHIPS.

You can get rid of tape worms and cure diarrhoea by eating the bark of the pomegranate tree.

3

Yugoslavia was first named Yugoslavia on 3 October 1929. The country's history is so mixed that today it is made up of six republics and five nationalities; and it has three religions and two alphabets.

Macedonian fishermen in Yugoslavia catch fish with trained cormorants. The birds have bands round their necks to prevent them swallowing the fish and when they return with the catch the fisherman simply removes it from their beaks.

THE BANK OF ENGLAND HAS ITS OWN WATER SUPPLY THAT IS PROVIDED BY AN ARTESIAN WELL.

On average we blink about twenty-five times a minute and each blink lasts about a fifth of a second.

October

4 The tiny African kingdom of Lesotho became independent on 4 October 1966. Lesotho has the highest lowest point on earth. That is to say that the lowest point in the country is still four-and-a-half thousand feet above sea-level.

Lesotho is one of the world leaders in the production of mohair wool from Angora goats.

IT IS ILLEGAL IN BRITAIN TO SELL A PET TO ANYONE UNDER THE AGE OF TWELVE.

The printing of the first edition of the Bible in English was completed on 4 October 1535. One edition of the Bible printed in 1631 omitted the word 'not' from the seventh commandment, so that it read, 'Thou shalt commit adultery.'

ONE HUNDRED YEARS AFTER STARTING BREWING THE BASS BREWERY WAS PRODUCING NEARLY ONE MILLION BARRELS OF BEER A YEAR.

5 The Arctic explorer, William Scoresby, was born on 5 October 1789. There are as many hours of light when a book can be read out of doors in the Arctic as there are in the tropics.

In the summer of 1934 an iceberg that had originated in the Arctic was spotted in the Atlantic on the latitude of the Canary Islands.

SOUND TRAVELS SO WELL IN THE ARCTIC THAT IT IS POSSIBLE TO LISTEN TO AN ORDINARY CONVERSATION THAT IS BEING CONDUCTED A MILE-AND-A-HALF AWAY.

Turkish baths are not baths and they did not originate in Turkey. They are rooms filled with hot air that were developed by the Romans.

October

6

The Poet Laureate, Alfred Lord Tennyson, died on 6 October 1892. Luckily for him he didn't depend on his salary as the Laureate when he was appointed to the position. In 1857 Queen Victoria's rat catcher was being paid more than her official poet.

The current Poet Laureate, Sir John Betjeman, has chosen to receive bottles of wine from the Royal wine merchant in preference to the compensation that has been paid since the end of the eighteenth century.

7

The first photograph of the dark side of the moon was taken on 7 October 1959, when the Russian spacecraft Lunik III flew behind the moon. The sun's corona only comes into view when the moon blots out the main body of the sun during a solar eclipse.

The Persian assembly was opened on 7 October 1906, by the Shah. Persia, or Iran as it is now, is the oldest country in the world. It has been independent for over 1,450 years.

CLEAN SNOW MELTS MORE SLOWLY THAN DIRTY SNOW.

Early Spaniards used to clean their teeth in urine.

October

8 Another male bastion fell on 8 October 1925, when a woman jockey won a race for the first time. The Newmarket Town Plate, which failed to specify the sex of the jockey when it was instituted by Charles II, allowed half a dozen lady jockeys to enter, one of whom won.

From over one thousand murders committed in Chicago during the last sixty years there have only been thirteen convictions.

THE THIRD EPISTLE OF ST. JOHN IS THE SHORTEST BOOK IN THE BIBLE.

Accents first appeared in the French language early in the seventeenth century.

THE OLDEST INHABITED CAPITAL CITY IN THE WORLD IS THE SYRIAN CAPITAL, DAMASCUS.

The goose-step, made famous by Hitler's troops, was first introduced into the British army.

9 Uganda became independent on 9 October 1962. The jaws of the African fire ant found in Uganda are sometimes used to tie together the sides of a wound instead of surgical stitches. The ant is made to bite both flaps of skin, then its body is twisted off and the jaws are left locked together to form a 'stitch'.

Sarah Bernhardt had the accident that eventually led to the amputation of her right leg while appearing in Tosca. She threw herself from the parapet of the castle, as demanded in the script. However, a slip-up in the stage-management had left her with nothing to land on but the bare stage and her right leg was never the same again.

SPIDERS NEVER SPIN COBWEBS ON CHESTNUT WOOD.

October

10

The great Italian operatic composer, Giuseppe Verdi, was born on 10 October 1813. One of his best loved works *Aida* gave another famous musician his big break. Arturo Toscanini once took the baton and conducted the whole of *Aida* from memory during a performance in South America. He had previously been playing the cello.

The Chinese Revolution broke out on 10 October 1911. During the Taiping rebellion, in the middle of the nineteenth century that lasted thirteen years, between twenty and thirty million Chinese were killed. The rebel leader thought that he was the younger brother of Jesus Christ.

WILLIAM III WAS THE FIRST ENGLISH MONARCH TO HAVE MORE THAN ONE BABTISMAL NAME.

It was quite common in ancient China for people to commit suicide by eating a pound of salt.

11

The Bohemian Hussite leader, John Ziska, died of the plague on 11 October 1424. He fought for the Teutonic Knights against the Poles, for the Austrians against the Turks and for the English against the French at the battle of Agincourt. He lost the sight of both eyes in battle but even so insisted on leading his troops into the fray, and when he eventually died he gave instructions that his skin was to be used to make a battle-drum to lead his troops into battle for evermore.

Eleanor Roosevelt, cousin and wife of President Franklin D. Roosevelt, was born on 11 October 1884. Her uncle, Theodore Roosevelt, had an inkwell that was made from the hollowed out foot of a rhinoceros.

THIRTEEN IS CONSIDERED A LUCKY NUMBER IN ITALY.

October

12 Today is Columbus Day in the U.S.A., commemorating the day on which Christopher Columbus discovered America. Almost one hundred of the sailors that made the epic voyage with him to the New World were convicts released straight from prison to make up numbers for the ships' crews.

Once he had discovered land to the west, Columbus was never shaken in his belief that he had found a new route to Asia. He was convinced that the island that he named San Salvador lay off the coast of Asia and that it was in fact part of Japan.

THE FIRST GOLD THAT COLUMBUS BROUGHT BACK FROM THE NEW WORLD WAS USED TO GILD THE CEILING OF THE CHURCH OF SANTA MARIA MAGGIORE.

The sphinx in Egypt is a statue of the goddess Armachis.

13 One of Edward VII's favourite mistresses, the actress Lillie Langtrey, was born on 13 October 1853. As well as her great success with men, she was popular with audiences too. Having once been found with a man in her hotel bedroom in St. Louis, while touring America, the theatre in which she was appearing broke box office records for the next fortnight.

Although Friday 13th is always regarded as unlucky, the thirteenth is more likely to fall on Friday than on any other day of the week.

BLOCKS OF TEA WERE USED AS CURRENCY IN SIBERIA UNTIL TWO HUNDRED YEARS AGO.

The female nine-banded armadillo is very precise about its babies. She either gives birth to four males or four females. There are always four babies of the same sex.

October

14

The battle of Hastings was fought on 14 October 1066. It wasn't a good day for the English King Harold as it was his birthday and the day he died.

The battle of Hastings wasn't actually fought at Hastings: it was fought seven miles away at Senlac Hill, near Pevensey.

OVER HALF THE BONES IN THE HUMAN SKELETON ARE IN THE WRISTS, ANKLES, HANDS AND FEET.

Dwight D. Eisenhower, American president and five star general, was born on 14 October 1890. As well as carrying the five pips of his rank on all his uniforms, he even had them sewn on to his pyjamas.

THE WHEELED TRANSPORT VEHICLE IS A THOUSAND YEARS OLDER THAN THE ROAD.

15

The Roman poet, Virgil, was born on 15 October 70 BC. His most famous work, the twelve-book-long epic, the *Aeneid*, was nearly lost to the world on his death. Virgil was such a stickler for perfection that he ordered the poem to be destroyed since he hadn't had time to polish it to his liking. Fortunately the Emperor Augustus, who had commissioned the work, ordered several other poets to make the few alterations that were necessary, and the *Aeneid* was published.

Virgil once spent the equivalent of £50,000 on the funeral of a favourite fly.

OF ALL THE LARGE BEASTS OF PREY THE LION HAS THE SMALLEST HEART.

Queen Victoria proposed to Prince Albert on 15 October 1839. She had to do the asking since the nervous young prince would never have dared to pop the question to the Queen of England.

October

16

Marie Antoinette, Queen of France, was guillotined on 16 October 1793. She and Jayne Mansfield shared the same bust measurement.

The Marquis De Pélier spent fifty years in prison as a result of committing a heinous crime against France's last queen. He whistled at her.

MONARCH BUTTERFLIES MIGRATE OVER 1,800 MILES EVERY YEAR.

There is a town in the department of Haute-Garonne in France that is simply called Oo.

SPRUNG SUSPENSION DIDN'T APPEAR IN PASSENGER COACHES UNTIL 1580.

17

Pontius Pilate is regarded as a saint in the Ethiopian church.

Kangaroo meat is cholesterol free.

THE POLISH ROMANTIC COMPOSER, FREDERIC CHOPIN, DIED ON 17 OCTOBER 1849. IN HIS ETUDE FOR PIANO IN G-FLAT MAJOR, THE *BLACK KEY ETUDE,* A WHITE KEY IS PLAYED ONLY ONCE.

Chopin got his inspiration for his Waltz No. 3 in F major from his cat, which ran across the keys of his piano. Chopin tried to copy the sound that it produced and nicknamed the piece The Cat's Waltz.

153

October

18 Lord Palmerston, former British Prime Minister and statesman, died on 18 October 1865, having told his physician only a short time before: "Die, my dear doctor? That's the last thing I shall do."

Henri Matisse's painting entitled Le Bateau *went on public display on 18 October 1961, in the Museum of Modern Art in New York. Large crowds flocked to see it, though many went away perplexed by the work; which wasn't surprising since it had been hung upside down, an error that wasn't spotted until forty-six days later.*

WHAT IS CONSIDERED TO BE THE IDEAL AMERICAN DIET WOULD KILL A MONKEY IN A VERY SHORT TIME.

Birds can sometimes set their own wings when they are broken.

◗◗◗◗◗◗◗◗◗◗◗◗◗◗◗◗◗◗◗◗◗◗◗◗◗◗◗◗◗◗◗◗

19 The British lost the American colonies on 19 October 1781, when General Cornwallis finally surrendered at Yorktown having run out of ammunition. During the American War of Independence though, more colonists had fought for the British than for the revolutionary army.

As it was, only sixteen per cent of the able bodied men in the American colonies actually took part in the American War of Independence.

A GERMAN POET NAMED HANS VON THUMMEL WAS BURIED IN THE HEART OF AN OAK TREE.

Britain and Egypt signed their agreement concerning the Suez Canal base on 19 October 1954. After the Arab-Israeli war of October 1973, both sides dug almost 700,000 land mines out of the banks on both sides of the canal.

A CHAMOIS CAN STAND ON AN AREA NOT MUCH
LARGER THAN A 50 PENCE PIECE.

October

20

The architect, Sir Christopher Wren, was born on 20 October 1632. Apart from designing St. Paul's Cathedral and sixty other buildings in London, Wren also devised a language for the deaf and dumb, which he claimed could be learned in less than an hour.

The most distant star in our galaxy is 75,000 light years from earth.

IF SUGAR IS ADDED TO CEMENT IT HELPS TO STRENGTHEN IT.

Lions and tigers are only 5-10 per cent successful in hunting their prey.

21

Alfred Nobel, the originator of the Nobel Prizes, was born on 21 October 1833. Ironically the man who established the world's most famous prize for peace made a small fortune from the manufacture of dynamite.

Samuel Taylor Coleridge, the poet and philosopher, was born on 21 October 1772. He was a prolific talker, often holding forth for hours on end. On one occasion his friend, Charles Lamb, was literally button-holed by Coleridge while they were walking one day. Coleridge took Lamb by one of his coat buttons, closed his eyes and started to discourse on the topic of the moment. After a while Lamb quietly cut the button from his coat and made his escape. He passed the point where he had left Coleridge, five hours later, and sure enough he was still talking there, with his eyes closed and the button held between his fingers.

ADMIRAL LORD HORATIO NELSON WAS KILLED AT THE BATTLE OF TRAFALGAR ON 21 OCTOBER 1805. HIS FLAGSHIP, *H.M.S. VICTORY*, HAD A CREW OF 850.

October

22

Franz Liszt, the composer who gave rise to the word Lisztomania, was born on 22 October 1811. Before he reached the age of twenty he had given concerts in every country in Europe except Norway and Sweden.

The largest opera house in the world, the Metropolitan Opera House in New York, was opened on 22 October 1883. Today it has a seating capacity of 3,800 people.

23

Today must rank as one of the most violent and bloodthirsty in history. Mark Antony and Octavius Caesar defeated Caesar's assassins Brutus and Cassius at the battle of Philippi on 23 October 42 BC. Oliver Cromwell won his first victory of the Civil War when the Royalist forces retreated at the battle of Edgehill on 23 October 1642. The battle of Caporetto began on 23 October 1917. Twenty-five years later to the day Montgomery launched his successful offensive against Rommel at the battle of El Alamein and on 23 October 1956, the Hungarian uprising broke out.

According to Archbishop James Usher, Archbishop of Armagh and former professor of Divinity at Trinity College, Dublin, God created the world on 23 October 4004 BC.

MORE PEOPLE ARE KICKED TO DEATH BY DONKEYS THAN DIE IN FLYING ACCIDENTS.

October

24 Zambia became independent on 24 October 1964. Zambia's biggest tourist attraction is the Victoria Falls, which has a water flow of over 70,000,000 gallons every minute.

The Danish astronomer Tycho Brahe died on 24 October 1601. As a young man he had lost his nose in a fight and for the rest of his life he wore an artificial nose made of gold and silver.

THE SPIRE OF SALISBURY CATHEDRAL LEANS NEARLY TWO FEET AWAY FROM THE PERPENDICULAR.

Centipedes have one pair of legs attached to every segment of their bodies.

AN IRISH BROGUE IS REALLY A TYPE OF SHOE.

Every year the arctic tern flies from the Arctic right round the world to the Antarctic and then back up to the Arctic again.

25 Two famous British battles were fought on St. Crispin's Day, 25 October. In the three-hour battle of Agincourt fought in 1415 nearly 1,500 French cavalry were killed. While 439 years later the Light Brigade made their famous charge at the battle of Balaclava during which 247 of the 673 men in the brigade were killed.

On 25 October 1599 the English Navy had a wonderful party. The admiral, Sir Edward Kennel, ordered eighty casks of brandy, nine of water, one of Malaga, 1,300 pounds of sugar, 25,000 limes, 80 pints of lemon juice and five pounds of nutmeg to be mixed for the brew. When it was ready it was served to the six thousand officers and men in the fleet.

PABLO PICASSO WAS BORN ON 25 OCTOBER 1881. DURING ONE MONTH IN 1936, HE PRODUCED NO LESS THAN TWENTY-THREE MAJOR OIL PAINTINGS.

October

26 On 26 October 1905, Sweden agreed to the repeal of the union of Sweden and Norway. Today the Swedes are the world's leading coffee drinkers. The daily coffee consumption in Sweden is nearly eleven times greater per person than it is in Great Britain.

The Swedes were also the first to use paper cartons exclusively for the sale of liquids like milk and fruit juice. Since 1969 glass milk bottles have completely disappeared in Sweden.

THERE IS ALMOST NO ILLITERACY IN SWEDEN. SINCE 1842 EVERY CHILD HAS HAD TO ATTEND SCHOOL FOR AT LEAST SEVEN YEARS.

The first genuine champagne was invented by a blind Benedictine monk named Dom Pierre Perignon. One of the world's most exclusive champagnes has been named after him.

27 Theodore Roosevelt, the twenty-fifth president of the U.S.A. was born on 27 October 1858. On New Year's Day, 1907, he shook hands with 8,513 people.

Theodore Roosevelt became the youngest president of the U.S.A. when he took office at the age of forty-two.

BOTH THEODORE ROOSEVELT'S WIFE AND MOTHER DIED ON THE SAME DAY.

The distance from the earth's crust to its centre has been calculated as being about the same as that from the North Pole to the capital of Iraq, Baghdad.

YOU NEED AS MUCH HEAT TO MELT A KILO OF SNOW AS YOU DO TO BOIL A LITRE OF SOUP AT ROOM TEMPERATURE.

The largest shadow that any of us is ever likely to see is the one cast by the earth on the surface of the moon during an eclipse.

October

28

Harvard College was founded on 28 October 1636. At that time it was surrounded by a tall stockade to keep out hostile Indians and wolves.

Until 1790 students were only admitted to the Harvard library three at a time.

THE RING-TAILED LEMUR MAKES THE SAME SOUND AS A CAT.

On 3 June 1891, The Sportsman *carried an account of a lucky traveller who saved his life with a bottle of Bass. The man was peacefully asleep when he was woken by the barking of his dog. Grabbing what he thought was his revolver he came face to face with a poisonous snake. On finding that he had a quart bottle of Bass in his hand and not a gun, the man smashed it across the snake's head and saved his own life.*

29

Sir Walter Raleigh was executed on 29 October 1613, after having spent the last thirteen years of his life confined in the Tower of London. After his execution his head was put into a red leather bag and was given to his wife who carried it with her for the rest of her life.

Mozart's masterpiece, Don Giovanni, *was performed for the first time on 29 October 1787. The composer wrote it at one sitting and it was played without rehearsal the following day.*

DDT HAD BEEN KNOWN FOR SIXTY YEARS BEFORE IT WAS FIRST USED.

Raleigh's History of the World *was Oliver Cromwell's favourite book, after the Bible.*

THERE ARE MANY BREEDS OF TROPICAL FISH THAT COULD SURVIVE IN AN AQUARIUM FILLED WITH HUMAN BLOOD.

October

30 On 30 October 1937, the earth had a near miss when a half-million ton asteroid shot past 485,000 miles from the earth's surface — a hair's breadth away in astronomical terms.

The Religious Society of Friends was given its more common name during a court case on 30 October 1650. George Fox, who had formed the new religious group, had told the magistrate to 'quake and tremble at the word of the Lord'. The magistrate retorted rather feebly that Fox made his followers 'Quakers', and the name has stuck ever since.

OAKS AND POPLARS ARE MORE COMMONLY STRUCK BY LIGHTNING THAN ANY OTHER TREES IN ENGLAND.

There was a fire at the Tower of London on 30 October 1841. Until 1789 lions had been used as guard 'dogs' at the Tower.

RACOONS OFTEN WASH THEIR FOOD BEFORE THEY EAT IT.

Snow crystals are hexagonal, although no two snowflakes have ever been found with exactly the same pattern of crystals.

31 Chiang Kai-Shek, the first president of Taiwan, was born on 31 October 1887. The island to which he and his supporters fled after the communist takeover of mainland China is half covered with forest.

Martin Luther nailed his '95 Theses' to the door of the church in Wittenberg and started the Reformation that split the Church in half, on 31 October 1517. By way of personal protest he later got married and sired six children.

HORSES CAN GO TO SLEEP STANDING UP.

The tropical tree called the Royal Poinciana, produces flowers before it produces leaves.

November

1

After four-and-half years lying on his back on top of scaffolding, Michelangelo unveiled the ceiling of the Sistine Chapel on 1 November 1512. He had painted much of the 5,808 square feet ceiling himself.

During the bitter fighting in the Pacific in the Second World War, the U.S. forces landed in the Solomon Islands on 1 November 1943. There is very little temperature range in the islands throughout the year. One set of figures shows December as being the coldest month with a temperature range of 70°-90°F and June-September as the coldest time of the year with a temperature range of exactly the same, 70°-90°F.

BEFORE MODERN CURRENCY CAME INTO USE, THE SOLOMON ISLANDERS USED DOGS' TEETH TO BUY AND SELL THEIR GOODS.

Peers of the realm cannot be arrested for civil offences. They can only be arrested for felony and treason.

ELEPHANTS CANNOT JUMP.

November

2

Jimmy Carter was elected president of the U.S.A. on 2 November 1976. He was the first U.S. president to be born in a hospital, all the others had been born at home.

Both North Dakota and South Dakota achieved statehood on 2 November 1889. Today each state has a smaller population than the District of Columbia around the capital Washington.

GEORGE BERNARD SHAW DIED ON 2 NOVEMBER 1950 AT THE AGE OF 94, AFTER BREAKING HIS LEG WHILE CUTTING A BRANCH OFF A TREE IN HIS GARDEN.

Only a year before he died, Shaw wrote Farfetched Fables, *a play about the future, which wasn't bad for a man of ninety-three.*

A BLIND, HANDICAPPED SCOTSMAN, WILLIAM McPHERSON, WAS ABLE TO READ WITH HIS TONGUE.

∞∞∞∞∞∞∞∞∞∞∞∞∞∞∞∞∞∞∞∞∞∞∞∞∞∞

3

Panama was proclaimed an independent state on 3 November 1903. Its most famous feature is of course the ship canal that links the Atlantic with the Pacific. What is generally less well-known is that due to the shape of the isthmus through which the canal is cut, ships sailing into the Pacific actually sail eastwards. The entrance on the Atlantic side is further west than the Pacific one.

Over 200,000,000 tons of rock and earth had to be removed to dig the fifty-mile-long canal.

WILLIAM THE CONQUEROR'S QUEEN, MATILDA, DIED ON 3 NOVEMBER 1083. SHE WAS THE SHORTEST QUEEN OF ENGLAND THERE HAS EVER BEEN, STANDING A MERE 4 FEET 2 INCHES.

We each breathe about four hundred cubic feet of air every twenty-four hours.

November

4

The first effective machine-gun was patented by Richard John Gatling on 4 November 1862. The deadly weapon, which was later developed to fire 1,200 rounds a minute, was in fact invented by a man who had, at one time, worked as a doctor in the American Civil War.

The German romantic-classical composer, Felix Mendelssohn, died on 4 November 1847. He was only seventeen when he wrote what has come to be one of his most popular works, the overture, A Midsummer Night's Dream.

AUGUSTE RODIN, ONE OF THE GIANTS OF NINE-TEENTH CENTURY SCULPTURE, WAS BORN ON 4 NOVEMBER 1840. ONE OF HIS MOST FAMOUS WORKS, *THE THINKER*, WAS ACTUALLY INTENDED TO BE A PORTRAIT OF THE POET DANTE.

5

William of Orange (William III) landed at Torbay on 5 November 1688, to replace the Stuart monarch, James II as King of England. This happened exactly eighty-three years to the day after Guy Fawkes and his accomplices had tried to blow up the Houses of Parliament and with them King James I, the first Stuart king, on 5 November 1605.

The cellars of the Palace of Westminster are still searched carefully before the opening of every parliament to ensure that no repetition of the Gunpowder Plot can take place.

UNTIL 1859 IT WAS ILLEGAL NOT TO CELEBRATE GUY FAWKES DAY.

There are some types of lichen that can absorb half their own weight of water in ten minutes.

THERE IS NO WORD IN ENGLISH THAT RHYMES WITH 'OBLIGE'.

November

6

Charles I's elder brother, Henry Frederick, Prince of Wales, died on 6 November 1612. For a long time there was great dispute over the cause of his death. But as scientific knowledge advanced it became clear that he was the first attested victim of typhoid.

Babies are only six times more active awake than when they are asleep.

ABRAHAM LINCOLN WAS ELECTED PRESIDENT OF THE UNITED STATES ON 6 NOVEMBER 1860. HE WAS THE FIRST U.S. PRESIDENT TO BE ASSASSINATED.

Lincoln wrote his famous Gettysburg address on the back of an envelope.

7

The great woman scientist, Marie Curie, was born on 7 November 1867. A pioneer of research into radioactivity, Marie Curie was the only woman to be awarded two Nobel prizes.

On 7 November 1631, Pierre Gassendi observed the transit of Mercury. This was the first time that the transit of a planet had been observed and recorded.

MERCURY'S YEAR IS HALF THE LENGTH OF ITS DAY. IT TAKES JUST UNDER EIGHTY-EIGHT EARTH DAYS TO REVOLVE ROUND THE SUN, BUT IT REVOLES VERY SLOWLY.

The guinea pig does not come from Guinea and it isn't a pig. It is a South American rodent.

November

Bram Stoker, the creator of Count Dracula, was born on 8 November 1847. Apparently the idea for his famous horror story came to him in a nightmare that he had after eating crabs for supper one night.

Our skeleton represents twenty per cent of our total body weight. Considering the strength of bones they are really very light. If we had steel bars of the same strength instead of bones, our skeletons would weigh over four times as much as they do.

THE BLIND POET, JOHN MILTON, DIED ON 8 NOVEMBER 1674. DURING HIS LIFETIME HE RECEIVED TEN POUNDS FOR HIS EPIC MASTERPIECE, *PARADISE LOST*.

Until the early 1800's burning at the stake was still a legal method of execution in many areas of the U.S.A.

CABBAGE IS 91 PER CENT WATER.

The man who created the kingdom of Saudi Arabia, Ibn Saud, died on 9 November 1953. Even though his country is the twelfth largest on earth, there is not a single river in it.

From the time that he was eleven until his death at the age of seventy-two it is said that Ibn Saud had sex with three different women every night, except during battles.

THE EMPTY QUARTER OF SAUDI ARABIA IS ONE OF THE LEAST EXPLORED AREAS IN THE WORLD AND YET IT COVERS AN AREA ONLY SLIGHTLY SMALLER THAN THE WHOLE OF NORWAY.

Cambodia became independent on 9 November 1953. There are seventy-two letters in the Cambodian alphabet.

November

10 The Gilbert and Ellice Islands (now **Kiribati and Tuvalu** respectively) were annexed by Britain on 10 November 1915. Although the land area of Kiribati is only 253 square miles, the total area of the territory, that is, the land and the sea together, is over two million square miles.

Tuvalu consists of nine atolls most of which are less than two miles wide and none of which is higher than fifteen feet above sea-level.

THE BRITISH USE ALMOST TWICE AS MUCH SOAP PER PERSON AS THE DUTCH.

Galileo's telescope was a less powerful instrument than most modern binoculars.

11 The First World War came to an end at the eleventh hour, of the eleventh day, of the eleventh month of 1918. Exactly sixty-five years later a cease-fire was agreed between Egypt and Israel.

Ned Kelly, the last of the Australian bushrangers, was hanged on 11 November 1880. Kelly always wore a suit of armour beaten out of ploughshares for his robberies and hold-ups.

ALMOST HALF THE WEALTH IN THE WORLD IS OWNED BY FOUR COUNTRIES WITH A TOTAL POPULATION THAT AMOUNTS TO UNDER FIFTEEN PER CENT OF THE WORLD'S POPULATION.

The Cenotaph was unveiled in Whitehall on 11 November 1920, yet twenty years later to the day the British Navy was attacking the Italian fleet in the harbour at Taranto.

ONE PARTICULAR TYPE OF GERMAN FLEA ONLY LIVES AND BREEDS INSIDE BEER MATS.

November

12

Alexander Borodin was born on 12 November 1834. He always called himself a 'musical amateur', which in some ways was true since in his spare time he was professor of chemistry at the Academy of Medicine in St. Petersburg.

Borodin took five years to complete his first symphony, seven to complete his second and he never finished his opera Prince Igor, *even though he had spent eighteen years working on it.*

IF A GLASS OF WATER WAS MAGNIFIED TO THE SIZE OF THE EARTH, THE INDIVIDUAL WATER MOLECULES WOULD BE THE SIZE OF AN ORANGE.

After killing their prey, leopards lift it up into trees to keep it away from other predators.

13

Robert Louis Stevenson, the author of *Treasure Island* **and** *Kidnapped,* **was born on 13 November 1850.**

Stevenson literally dreamt up the plot of his horror story, Dr Jekyll and Mr Hyde. *The plot came to him in a dream and it took him only six days to write and then rewrite the whole book.*

ACCORDING TO MEDICAL EVIDENCE WE SNORE LESS WHILE WE ARE DREAMING.

Rice paper is not made from rice. It is either made from pitch or wood-pulp.

THE EARTH REVOLVES AROUND THE SUN ABOUT EIGHT TIMES FASTER THAN THE VELOCITY AT WHICH A BULLET LEAVES A GUN.

When measured by volume alone all the gold that has ever been mined on earth would only equal the amount of steel produced every two hours in the U.S.A.

November

○○○○○○○○○○○○○○○○○○○○○○○○○○○○○○○○○

14

Prince Charles was born on 14 November 1948. Amongst his many possessions, he owns the Oval cricket ground and the site of Dartmoor Prison.

Princess Anne married Captain Mark Phillips on her brother's twenty-fifth birthday. That very afternoon one of the winning horses at the Wolverhampton race meeting was named 'Royal Mark'.

THE PIONEER OF STEAMBOATS, ROBERT FULTON, WAS BORN ON 14 NOVEMBER 1765. THE INVENTIVE STREAK RAN DEEP IN HIS FAMILY, FOR IT WAS ONE OF HIS DESCENDANTS WHO INVENTED THE BRA AND WHO TOOK OUT A PATENT ON IT.

○○○○○○○○○○○○○○○○○○○○○○○○○○○○○○○○○

15

Brazil became independent on 15 November 1889. The plant called the *bencas de dios* **is grown as a vegetable in Brazil but in France the same plant is called** *abutillon* **and is only used for flower decorations.**

18,000 of all the known species of plants grow in the Amazon Basin.

THE SUPREME COURT JUDGE, FELIX FRANKFURTER, WAS BORN ON 15 NOVEMBER 1882. THE FRANKFURTER SAUSAGE WAS INVENTED IN CHINA.

Botanically, rhubarb is a vegetable while cucumbers, pumpkins and tomatoes are really fruits.

THERE IS A LAKE ON THE ISLAND OF JAVA THAT BLOWS BUBBLES INTO THE AIR.

One of the more unusual ancient cosmetics was one devised by Nero's wife, Poppea, who used to preserve her beauty by applying a face-mask of bread crumbs and asses milk each night.

November

16

If the human voice could carry through the air for great distances without decreasing in volume, it would take fourteen hours for a shout bellowed in Australia to be heard on the west coast of the U.S.A.

The British captured Fort Washington on 16 November 1776. Today no building may be built in the city of Washington D.C. that is higher than the Capitol building.

THERE ARE ONLY TWO TYPES OF MOUSE FOUND IN IRELAND.

The Emperor Tiberius was born on 16 November 42 BC. He was so strong that he could poke a finger through an apple.

17

The Polish constitution was established on 17 November 1921. Poland had not existed as an independent country for 150 years before foreign rule ended after the First World War.

Mary I, Queen of England, died on 17 November 1558, after an uninspiring reign that saw religious turmoil at home and the loss of England's last possession in France, Calais.

BARON DOMINIQUE LARREY, NAPOLEON BONAPARTE'S PRIVATE SURGEON, COULD AMPUTATE A MAN'S LEG IN FOURTEEN SECONDS.

The third hand on a watch is the second hand.

KIWIS LAY EGGS THAT CAN WEIGH AS MUCH AS ONE QUARTER OF THEIR TOTAL BODY WEIGHT.

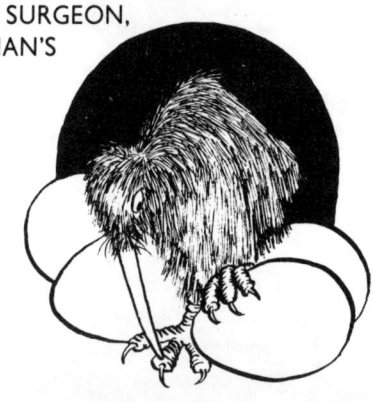

November

18   **W.S. Gilbert was born on 18 November 1836. Two years later he was kidnapped and a ransom of £25 had to be paid before he was released. This childhood episode appeared in two of his operettas that he wrote with Sullivan:** *The Gondoliers* **and** *The Pirates of Penzance.*

Mickey Mouse made his first appearance on 18 November 1928. Mickey has only got four fingers on each hand.

THE LAST MULES EMPLOYED BY THE BRITISH ARMY WENT INTO RETIREMENT IN 1975.

19   **Abraham Lincoln gave his famous address at Gettysburg on 19 November 1863. Commenting on his immortal closing words, "that government of the people, by the people, for the people, shall not perish from the earth",** *The Times* **in London commented, "Anything more dull and commonplace it would not be easy to reproduce."**

THE SURNAME OF THE LEGENDARY LIBERATOR OF SWITZERLAND, WILLIAM TELL, MEANS 'THE MAD'.

20   **King George V's eldest daughter, the then Princess Elizabeth, married Lieutenant Philip Mountbatten on 20 November 1947. Amongst the thousands of wedding presents they received were 32,000 food parcels sent from well-wishers in America.**

The great Russian novelist, Leo Tolstoy, died on 20 November 1910. After witnessing a public execution in Paris he was so appalled that he vowed never to serve again under any form of government.

November

21 One of Cole Porter's greatest Broadway successes opened on 21 November 1934 in such a rush that a title hadn't been properly settled on and in the end in was billed as *Anything Goes*.

The writer and philosopher, Voltaire, was born on 21 November 1694. Throughout his life he felt the cold and he insisted that he had a fire in his study every day of the year.

GORILLAS CANNOT SWIM.

The first country to legalize abortion was the U.S.S.R. where abortions ceased to be illegal in 1920.

THE STARFISH HAS AN EYE ON THE END OF EACH OF ITS ARMS.

22 President John F. Kennedy was shot in Dallas on 22 November 1963. He was one of only two U.S. presidents to be outlived by their fathers. The other one was President Harding.

President Kennedy was a phenomenal reader, he used to be able to read four newspapers in twenty minutes.

MIGRATING SWALLOWS TAKE ABOUT A MONTH TO FLY FROM ENGLAND TO AFRICA.

The Olympic Games opened in Melbourne on 22 November 1956. Among the many distinguished winners of Olympic medals are two European kings. Both King Olav of Norway and King Constantine of Greece won gold medals for sailing.

OUR NERVES TRANSMIT MESSAGES AT A SPEED OF ABOUT 300 FT/SEC.

The first recorded use of 'dwindle', 'hurry', and 'lonely' are in the works of William Shakespeare.

November

23

On 23 November 1942, Second Steward Poon Lim of the Merchant Navy began his 133-day survival on a raft after his ship was torpedoed. Four-and-a-half months later he was rescued off the coast of Brazil after drifting alone in the Atlantic.

TERMITES CAN PRODUCE SUBSTANCES IN THEIR BODIES THAT CAN RUST STEEL, BURN THROUGH LEAD AND DISINTEGRATE GLASS.

Harpo Marx, the silent one of the Marx Brothers, was born on 23 November 1893. Among his many little curiosities was the habit of greeting guests stark naked to see what their reaction would be.

THE EARLIEST JUKEBOX WAS INSTALLED IN A BAR ON 23 NOVEMBER 1889. IT CONSISTED OF AN EDISON PHONOGRAPH WITH FOUR LISTENING TUBES.

24

A storm of controversy followed the publication of Darwin's *Origin of Species* on 24 November 1859. The storm was still rumbling thirty-five years later. For, when the spire of St. Mary's Church, Shrewsbury, collapsed in 1894, the rector told his congregation that it had been cast down because they had been raising funds for a memorial to Darwin, a Shrewsbury man.

The transit of Venus was first observed by Jeremiah Horrocks on 24 November 1639. Venus is one of only two planets without any apparent satellites. The other planet is Mercury.

KING LOUIS XIII OF FRANCE AND ANNE OF AUSTRIA WERE MARRIED ON 24 NOVEMBER 1615. THEY WERE BOTH FOURTEEN AT THE TIME.

November

25 Pierre de Coubertin proposed the revival of the Olympic Games on 25 November 1892. The first modern Olympics were held in Athens in 1896 with nine nations taking part.

AT THE WINTER OLYMPICS HELD IN CHAMONIX, FRANCE IN 1924, CURLING WAS INCLUDED AS A GOLD MEDAL EVENT.

At the 1900 Olympic regatta an unnamed French boy coxed a Dutch crew and won a gold medal with them. The boy was less than ten years old.

IN NOVEMBER 1894 *LICENSING WORLD* CARRIED AN ARTICLE ADVISING SUFFERERS FROM GOUT WHAT THEY SHOULD OR SHOULD NOT DRINK. DR MAPOTHER, WHO IS QUOTED IN THE ARTICLE, ADVISED GOUT SUFFERERS TO DRINK BASS INDIA DRAUGHT PALE ALE, AS IN HIS VIEW IT WAS LAXATIVE, AND DID NOT DISAGREE WITH THEIR COMPLAINT.

26 Karl Benz, the inventor of the motor car, was born on 26 November 1844. His first car appeared on the road in 1885. The first all-British car, the Lanchester, was made in 1895.

Brakes on all four wheels of a car didn't become a normal feature until the 1920's.

UNTIL 1920, IT WAS UNUSUAL FOR TRUCKS TO DRIVE FASTER THAN 10 MPH.

Britain's first stretch of motorway was opened near Preston in 1958.

RHUBARB GETS ITS NAME FROM THE WORD IN ANCIENT GREEK FOR THE RIVER VOLGA.

November

27 Spain established a protectorate in Morocco on 27 November 1912. It is possible to see snow on trees in Morocco, even in the height of summer. The trees are in the high Atlas mountains.

The University of Karueein, in the Moroccan city of Fez, was established in 859 and is believed to be the oldest teaching establishment in the world.

THE CITY OF MARRAKESH IS BUILT ALMOST ENTIRELY OUT OF RED MUD.

Bishop Francis Godwin described the sensation of weightlessness that is experienced on a journey to the moon in a book that he wrote in 1638.

EVERY SIKH IS CALLED *SINGH*, THE INDIAN WORD WHICH MEANS LION-HEARTED.

28 Albania achieved its independence on 28 November 1912. One fifteenth century king of Albania, named Scanderburg, once executed two prisoners by binding them together and then cutting them both in half at the waist with one blow from his sword.

The desert country of Mauritania became an independent country on 28 November 1960. Over forty per cent of the country is covered by moving sand dunes.

MAURITANIA IS ONE OF THE EMPTIEST COUNTRIES ON EARTH. THERE ARE FEWER THAN FOUR PEOPLE LIVING IN EVERY SQUARE MILE OF THE COUNTRY.

Blue eyes have less pigment than brown eyes.

November

29 Britain and France agreed to develop the supersonic airliner Concorde on 29 November 1962. At the beginning of 1980 one Concorde flew from New York to London in a record time that was forty-six seconds short of three hours.

The dashing leader of the Royalist cavalry during the Civil War, Prince Rupert, died on 29 November 1682. After the Restoration of his cousin, Charles II, Rupert devoted his time to his pet hobby, science, and before his death he had developed a method of mezzotint engraving, made improvements in the manufacture of gunpowder, invented an alloy of zinc and copper and had found a new way of boring cannon.

THE GIANT SQUID HAS EYES THAT MEASURE OVER A FOOT IN DIAMETER.

Egyptian musicians were playing harps and flutes six thousand years ago.

30 The U.S.S.R. invaded Finland on 30 November 1940. Finland is the most thickly forested country in Europe, with nearly two-thirds of the country covered with trees.

An international treaty forbids the Finnish airforce from having any bombers or any aircraft capable of carrying bombs.

THE GULF OF FINLAND FREEZES OVER FOR BETWEEN FOUR AND SIX MONTHS EVERY YEAR, DEPENDING ON HOW SEVERE THE WINTER IS.

Sir Winston Churchill was born on 30 November 1874. Following his escape from a Boer prison-camp during the Boer War in 1899, a price of £25 was placed on his head, dead or alive.

175

December

1

Lady Astor, Britain's first woman M.P. took her seat in the House of Commons on 1 December 1919. However, even she couldn't really claim to be the first British woman to sit in the House of Commons since she was actually born in America.

Henry I died as a result of eating too many lampreys on 1 December 1135. It was thanks to him that we inherited the measurements of length that we have today, for it was he who decreed that a yard was to equal the distance from the end of his thumb to the end of his nose.

IT'S RECKONED THAT HENRY I SIRED AS MANY AS TWENTY ILLEGITIMATE CHILDREN.

The correct scientific name for a werewolf is a 'lycanthrope'.

IN THE VERY COLD WINTER OF 1890-1 IT WAS POSSIBLE TO SKATE ALL THE WAY FROM LECHLADE, IN GLOUCESTERSHIRE, TO LONDON, DOWN THE FROZEN RIVER THAMES.

The Hundred Years War actually lasted 114 years.

One famous eighteenth century gourmet named Anthelme Brillat-Savarin was born in a town with a very appropriate name. It was called Belley.

BACH ONCE WROTE A CANTATA ABOUT COFFEE.

December

2

The United Arab Emirates became independent on 2 December 1971. Four years later the tiny oil state was buying goods from the west with cheerful abandon. Among items bought were 1,800 tons of sand, that went to Abu Dhabi from England, and a snow-plough.

The world's first nuclear pile started to operate on 2 December 1942. Although the output was only half a watt at first, the power produced by the pile increased four hundred times in just ten days.

THE MARQUIS DE SADE DIED ON 2 DECEMBER 1814. IN *ONE HUNDRED DAYS OF SODOM* HE CATALOGUED SIX HUNDRED DIFFERENT WAYS OF HAVING SEX.

Morris dancing probably originated in Spain.

CAKES WERE ORIGINALLY ICED WITH A BUNCH OF FEATHERS

3

Pierre Auguste Renoir died on 3 December 1919. During the closing months of his life the great artist was so crippled with arthritis that he couldn't use his hands at all. This didn't prevent him from painting however, he had the brushes tied to his arms and continued to paint.

Napoleon Bonaparte captured Madrid on 3 December 1808. In spite of his dislike of the English, Napoleon was a great admirer of industrial expertise. He always insisted on shaving with an English razor for example, because he maintained that these were greatly superior to French razors.

WILD APPLE JUICE WILL REMOVE WARTS.

The novelist, Joseph Conrad, was born in Poland on 3 December 1857. In the early part of his working life he was a smuggler.

December

4

The philosopher, Thomas Hobbes, died on 4 December 1679. When he was eighty-four, seven years before his death, he wrote his autobiography — in Latin verse.

The Scottish historian and essayist, Thomas Carlyle, was born on 4 December 1795. A man of remarkable memory, Carlyle had to completely rewrite the first volume of his History of the French Revolution *from memory, after his manuscript had been used to light a fire by the servant of the friend to whom he had lent it.*

THE ONLY TIMES WHEN A QUEEN BEE LEAVES HER HIVE IS TO LEAD OUT HER SWARM OR TO GO ON HER WEDDING FLIGHT.

New York City's Empire State Building was built to be able to withstand a sway of one foot from the perpendicular.

5

The union of Ghana and British Togoland was approved on 5 December 1956. Ghana is the world's largest exporter of cocoa, the second largest producer of rough diamonds and the sixth largest producer of gold, which explains why it was originally called the Gold Coast.

Over one hundred and fifty different types of tree grow in the forests of Ghana.

ANY STURGEON THAT IS CAUGHT IN BRITISH WATERS BECOMES THE PROPERTY OF THE REIGNING MONARCH AND ANY CAVIAR FROM THE FISH ENDS UP ON THE ROYAL DINNER-TABLE.

When kaleidoscopes were first invented in 1816 they were intended to help textile designers with their work.

December

6

Thomas Alva Edison made the first recording of sound on 6 December 1877, when he spoke into his 'talking machine' and after a few adjustments, the machine talked back. The first words that were ever recorded were: "Mary had a little lamb".

Today is the feast day of St. Nicholas, the patron saint of merchants, thieves, pawnborkers, sailors, virgins and even Russia.

FINLAND WAS PROCLAIMED INDEPENDENT ON 6 DECEMBER 1917. THE FINNISH LANGUAGE HAS OVER FOUR THOUSAND IRREGULAR VERBS.

The largest electric eels can produce electric shocks powerful enough to kill a man.

BY 1944 WAR EXPENDITURE IN BRITAIN HAD REACHED THE LEVEL OF OVER £1,000,000,000 A WEEK.

7

The U.S.A. declared war on Austria-Hungary on 7 December 1917 and exactly twenty-four years later it was at war again when the Japanese attacked Pearl Harbour crippling the American Pacific Fleet and destroying two hundred aircraft on the ground.

Today is the feast day of St. Ambrose, a fourth century Bishop of Milan, who was the first to make use of hymns in worship and who probably wrote several hymns that are still in use today.

WHEN QUEEN ANNE DIED SHE WAS SO SWOLLEN WITH DROPSY THAT SHE HAD TO BE BURIED IN A SQUARE COFFIN.

The emperor Nero used to eat large quantities of leeks in the hope that they would improve his singing voice.

December

8   **Henry Jenkins died at Ellerton, in Yorkshire, on 8 December 1670, at the reputed age of 169. Although he was often accused of being a fraud, he was able to describe life in Tudor England with amazing accuracy and he used to give a very convincing account of the battle of Flodden (1513), at which he claimed to have fought.**

Britain and the U.S.A. declared war on Japan on 8 December 1941. The Japanese emperor Hirohito is the 124th emperor of Japan and is a direct descendant of the first emperor Jimmu Tenno, who reigned 2,000 years ago.

THE MOST POWERFUL TELESCOPE IN THE WORLD COULD DETECT A CANDLE 15,000 MILES AWAY.

9   **John Milton was born on 9 December 1608. Although known today for his fine poetry, Milton spent twenty years of his life almost exclusively engaged in writing revolutionary manifestos in prose.**

Thomas Topham, an eighteenth century English strongman, could snap his fingers while a man jumped up and down on each of his outstretched arms.

A TWENTY-FIVE-YEAR-OLD WOMAN HAS ABOUT THE SAME MUSCULAR POWER AS A SIXTY-FIVE-YEAR-OLD MAN.

Dame Edith Sitwell died on 9 December 1964. In 1922 she and her brother read their poems through a huge mask that filled the centre of the stage where they were performing.

December

The American poetess, Emily Dickinson, was born on 10 December 1830. When she grew up she thought she was so ugly that whenever anyone called on her, she used to sit in another room and talk to them through an open door.

Cuba became an independent state on 10 December 1898. Cuba was actually ruled by Britain for one year of its history (1762-63) but the British clearly didn't think much of the island and swapped it with Spain in exchange for Florida.

IN 1968 THERE WAS A THUNDERSTORM OVER LAPLEAU IN FRANCE IN WHICH LIGHTNING STRUCK A FLOCK OF SHEEP, KILLING ALL THE BLACK ONES BUT LEAVING THE WHITE SHEEP UNHARMED.

11

The uncrowned king, Edward VIII, abdicated on 11 December 1936. He is the only British king to have written an autobiography.

Edward VIII's predecessor as Prince of Wales, Edward VII, kept a fireman's uniform waiting for him at Charing Cross Fire Station so that he could attend any important fires.

COCKCROACHES HAVE REMAINED UNCHANGED FOR ABOUT 250,000,000 YEARS.

Indiana achieved statehood on 11 December 1816. However, it's not a good place to live if you happen to enjoy continental cooking. There is a law in the state which makes it illegal to ride on a bus within four hours of eating garlic.

BRITISH BARRISTERS STILL WEAR MOURNING FOR QUEEN MARY WHO DIED IN 1694.

Brushes used to apply varnish last nearly a hundred times longer than brushes used to apply paint.

December

12 Kenya became independent on 12 December 1963. Members of the Luo tribe in Kenya identify themselves by removing six of their lower teeth at the front of their mouths.

The baobab tree which grows to a huge size in Kenya is sometimes used as a house. Very old baobab trees are hollowed out and turned into homes by the tribesmen.

BARN OWLS CAN SEE 100 TIMES BETTER AT NIGHT THAN HUMAN BEINGS.

Sir Christopher Cockerell patented the hovercraft on 12 December 1955 after conducting experiments with pieces of household equipment like a vacuum-cleaner, a set of kitchen scales, a tin of coffee and a tin of cat food.

THE INDIAN CHENCHU TRIBE BELIEVE THAT NIGHTIME SEX PRODUCES BLIND CHILDREN.

13 Dr Johnson died on 13 December 1784. One of his earliest memories was of being touched by Queen Anne when he was suffering from scrofula, the 'king's disease'.

Johnson's best known work is his dictionary, which contained the definitions of 40,000 English words. The dictionary was a masterpiece of scholarship that occupied its compiler for eight years. Even so it did contain some strange glosses, like the one for oats: "A grain which in England is generally given to horses, but in Scotland supports the people".

IT TAKES OVER 140,000 CROCUSES TO MAKE ONE KILO OF SAFFRON.

The rainbow trout makes its nest from pebbles that it carries in its mouth.

December

14

Women voted for the first time in a British General Election on 14 December 1918. Women in New Zealand were given the right to vote as early as 1893; while Swiss women had to wait until 1971 before they could express their opinions at the ballot box.

George Washington died on 14 December 1799. Among the many sets of false teeth he had tried in his life were ones made from elm and another made from hippopotamus ivory.

AMERICA'S FIRST PRESIDENT HAD A FACE THAT WAS BADLY SCARRED BY SMALLPOX.

In the twenty-five years between 1750 and 1775 the exports of beer from the port of Hull rose by a staggering 1,490 per cent. Well over half of that increase was accounted for by beer brewed in Burton.

EAU DE COLOGNE WAS ORIGINALLY DEVELOPED AS A MEANS OF PROTECTION AGAINST THE PLAGUE.

15

The engineer and designer of the most famous feature of the Parisian skyline, Gustav Eiffel, was born on 15 December 1832. In 1905 a man ran up the 729 steps of the Eiffel Tower in 3 minutes 12 seconds.

As well as designing the tower that bears his name, Eiffel also designed the steel interior skeleton of the Statue of Liberty.

HENRY FORD ONCE TRIED TO BUY THE EIFFEL TOWER AND HAVE IT SHIPPED BACK TO THE U.S.A.

In 1726 Charles Sanson inherited his father's post at the age of six. His father had been Chief Executioner of Paris.

BETWEEN 1766 AND 1795 THE PUPILS OF WINCHESTER COLLEGE REBELLED ON THREE OCCASIONS.

December

16

Beethoven was born on 16 December 1770. After he became totally deaf, the great composer attempted to 'hear' what he was playing by placing a little stick on the top of his piano and biting on it.

AT TIMES WHEN HE WAS HAVING DIFFICULTY WITH A COMPOSITION BEETHOVEN USED TO POUR ICED WATER OVER HIS HEAD TO STIMULATE HIS BRAIN.

Beethoven was completely deaf when he composed his last and greatest symphony, the ninth.

17

Man took to the air with a sustained powered flight on 17 December 1903, when Orville Wright flew the *Flyer* over the beach at Kitty Hawk, North Carolina. This first powered flight lasted twelve seconds.

Lord Kelvin, a leading nineteenth century scientist, died on 17 December 1907. He once proved mathematically that it was impossible to fly in a heavier-than-air machine.

FOR THIRTY-SIX YEARS OF HIS LIFE ST. SIMEON THE STYLITE LIVED AT THE TOP OF A PILLAR SIXTY FEET HIGH.

December

18

Joseph Grimaldi, the great nineteenth century clown, was born on 18 December 1779. He was the first clown to give himself a white face, and since his time every clown with a white face has been called Joey in his honour.

The star of the 1939 film Million Dollar Legs, *Betty Grable, was born on 18 December 1916. Ironically her legs were insured for that sum, making them probably the most valuable limbs ever.*

THE EGYPTIANS KEPT DACHSUNDS AS PETS FOUR THOUSAND YEARS AGO.

Elizabeth of Russia was born on 18 December 1709. During her lifetime she collected no fewer than 15,000 dresses.

ASSUMING THAT A DAY IS THE TIME BETWEEN SUNRISE AND SUNSET, ONE DAY IN SUMMER ON SPITZBERGEN LASTS THREE AND A HALF MONTHS.

On stage, peacocks' feathers and any reference to peacocks are considered bad luck.

19

The landscape painter, Joseph Turner, died on 19 December 1851. Turner's unique technique was developed through a number of curious methods. He painted his famous picture of *The Snowstorm* after taking to sea in a violent storm and ordering the skipper to lash him to the mast so that he could experience the fury of the elements at first hand.

Every year the ocean level in the northern hemisphere drops by slightly under eight inches. However, there does not appear to be a corresponding rise in the southern hemisphere's ocean level and no one has yet explained where the water goes.

December

○○○○○○○○○○○○○○○○○○○○○○○○○○○○○○○○○○

20 Peter the Great of Russia reformed the Russian calendar on 20 December 1699. He was a man of immense strength who could break silver coins with his fingers.

Peter the Great had such a hate for the Kremlin, which had been the scene of the murder of his mother's family, that he built a new capital, St. Petersburg and refused to carry out any repairs at all in Moscow.

A MEDIUM-SIZED SWARM OF LOCUSTS CONTAINS ABOUT A MILLION INSECTS WHICH CAN EAT TWENTY TONS OF FOOD BETWEEN THEM IN A DAY.

There are over 50,000 earthquakes on earth every year, although most of them are too small to be noticed.

○○○○○○○○○○○○○○○○○○○○○○○○○○○○○○○○○○

21 Dick Whittington's will was published on 21 December 1423. The real man behind the pantomime character lived a fairy-tale story almost as amazing as the one on the stage. He was a wealthy businessman who managed to become acting Mayor of London, a knight and a creditor to the King, all while still in his teens.

Benjamin Disraeli was born on 21 December 1804. Throughout his life he slept in a bed which had its feet in bowls of salt water to ward off evil spirits.

DISRAELI WAS A BEST-SELLING NOVELIST BEFORE HE DECIDED TO TURN HIS HAND TO POLITICS.

Clogs are usually carved out of alder wood.

LORD'S CRICKET GROUND IN LONDON WAS ORIGINALLY IN DORSET SQUARE

December

22 An unusual looking fish, five feet long, was dredged out of the sea off the coast of South Africa on 22 December 1938. The fish was later identified as a coelacanth, a prehistoric fish that had lived 400,000,000 years ago and which was thought to have become extinct 70,000,000 years ago.

The lungfish which is another prehistoric hangover (it was known to be on the earth 200,000,000 years ago) can live out of the water in a state of suspended animation for three years.

MILK IS HEAVIER THAN CREAM.

Mary Ann Evans, one of the greatest writers of the English novel, died on 22 December 1880. Mary Ann Evans was better known by her masculine name, George Eliot.

∞∞∞∞∞∞∞∞∞∞∞∞∞∞∞∞∞∞∞∞∞∞∞∞

23 The U.S. Federal Reserve Bank was founded on 23 December 1913. The U.S. Mint once made the unfortunate mistake of printing a run of gold coins with the words 'In Gold We Trust'. Though this may in fact have been perfectly true, the 'I' in 'Gold' should not have been included.

Inflation soared during the American War of Independence. The price of flour rose 15,000 per cent and the price of beef rose 33,000 per cent.

HITLER AND OTHER NAZI LEADERS STILL HAVE OVER ONE MILLION DOLLARS INVESTED IN AMERICAN BANKS.

During the early days of the California Gold Rush speculators could pay nearly £3.50 for a glass of whisky in San Francisco.

THE REDWOOD TREE HAS FIREPROOF BARK.

December

24
Howard Hughes was born on 24 December 1905. An enigmatic man for the closing years of his life, Hughes once had his hair cut by a barber and insisted that the man use three dozen combs and a new scissors made of German soligen steel.

Howard Hughes once wrote four pages of notes about Jane Russell's bosom.

25
Three royal figures ascended to their regal status on Christmas Day. On Christmas Day 800 Pope Leo III crowned Charlemagne the first Holy Roman Emperor. Two hundred and sixty-six years later William the Conqueror was crowned King of England, and on 25 December 1921, Emperor Hirohito of Japan acceded to his throne.

ALTHOUGH CHRISTMAS DAY IS USUALLY ASSOCIATED WITH SNOW, LONDON HAS ONLY HAD SEVEN WHITE CHRISTMASES THIS CENTURY.

There is no evidence to suggest that either Jesus Christ or the prophet Mohammed were able to write.

IN HEBREW THE WORD JESUS MEANS 'SAVIOUR' AND CHRIST MEANS 'ANNOINTED'.

26
Former U.S. President, Harry S. Truman, died on 26 December 1972. During his 1948 campaign to win the presidency, Truman travelled 31,000 and gave 356 speeches in the space of thirty-five days.

When heroin was discovered in Germany in the late 1890's many people believed that a cure for opium addiction had been found, at last.

December

27

The aged prophetess, Joanna Southcott, died on 27 December 1814. Shortly before her death she announced that she was pregnant with the second coming of Christ and promptly proved the point by eating 160 asparagus heads at one sitting.

The essayist, Charles Lamb, died on 27 December 1834, after a care-worn life spent looking after his sister Mary. Mary spent half of her life in a straight jacket and the other half entertaining Charles's literary friends like Coleridge, Hazlitt and de Quincey. During one of her earlier psychotic attacks Mary had stabbed her own mother to death.

THE DEEPEST MINE ON EARTH COULD ACCOMODATE EIGHT BUILDINGS THE HEIGHT OF THE EMPIRE STATE BUILDING PILED ON TOP OF EACH OTHER.

Peter Pan opened at the Duke of York's Theatre for the first time on 27 December 1904. The first Captain Hook was the father of the novelist, Daphne du Maurier.

December

28 The former President of the U.S.A., Woodrow Wilson, was born on 28 December 1856. He is the only president in the history of his country to have held a Ph.D. degree.

The first public office that Woodrow Wilson ever held was that of governor of New Jersey. Yet less than two years later he found himself president of the most powerful country on earth.

ABOUT ONE TENTH OF THE EARTH'S SURFACE IS COVERED BY GLACIERS, AN AREA THAT ROUGHLY CORRESPONDS TO THE WHOLE OF SOUTH AMERICA.

The first time that liquid fuel was used to power a rocket was in 1948.

THE HAIRS IN A MAN'S BEARD ARE ABOUT AS STRONG AS COPPER WIRES OF THE SAME DIMENSION.

29 Texas achieved its statehood on 29 December 1845. Everything is big in Texas. One ranch there, the King Ranch, lives up to its name by covering one and a quarter million acres.

Many of the black slaves who had formerly worked on Texan ranches went to work in the wild west in the second-half of the last century, which accounts for the fact that nearly one cowboy in three was either Mexican or black.

THERE IS AN ARCHIPELAGO IN FINLAND THAT HAS 30,000 ISLANDS.

When Apollo X re-entered the earth's atmosphere in 1969 the crew were travelling at a speed of 24,790.8 mph, faster than man had ever flown before.

THERE IS AN INLET IN THE SOUTH ISLAND OF NEW ZEALAND CALLED DOUBTFUL SOUND

December

30

The writer, Rudyard Kipling, was born on 30 December 1865. After he had written one of the best English short stories, *The Man Who Would be King,* he was sacked from his job on a San Francisco paper by the editor, who told him that he didn't know how to use the English language.

One of the pioneers of women's rights died on 30 December 1894. She attempted to liberate women by wearing trousers that exposed two inches of her ankles. The name of the good lady was Amelia Jenks Bloomer, and her daring new garments have been named after her ever since.

ONLY A MOTHER CAN BE CHARGED WITH INFANTI-CIDE. ANYONE ELSE WHO KILLS A CHILD IS CHARGED WITH MURDER.

Until 1970 it was against the law to play the drums in Oman.

31

Today is the last day of the year and Hogmanay in Scotland, a word which probably comes from the Norman French word which used to be shouted as a greeting — *Aguillanneuf.*

The last pub in the Faroe Islands closed on 31 December 1918.

A SO-CALLED TEN GALLON HAT ACTUALLY HOLDS NO MORE THAN 6 PINTS.

Louis XV of France had the motto Ultima ratis regum engraved on his cannon. Translated it means 'the last argument of kings'.

ONE OF CHARLES II'S FAVOURITE CHEFS, GILES ROSE, ONCE WROTE A BOOK GIVING INSTRUCTIONS ON HOW TO FOLD TABLE NAPKINS INTO TWENTY-SIX DIFFERENT SHAPES.

HAPPY NEW YEAR!

Amazing Challenge

If you have discovered a piece of amazing information that is both provable and relates to a specific day of the year, please send it to us so that we can consider it for the next edition of the Carling Black Label *Amazing Almanac*. Each piece of information should be submitted on this form or a copy of it and all submissions should be sent by 30 June 1982. The person supplying the piece of information that Gyles Brandreth judges to be the most amazing will be rewarded with a year's supply of Carling Black Label. If you are under the age of eighteen you will receive an alternative reward.

NAME:

ADDRESS:

DAYTIME TELEPHONE NO. (if any):

DATE OF BIRTH:

THE AMAZING INFORMATION:

DAY OF THE YEAR YOU THINK THE AMAZING INFORMATION SHOULD FEATURE ON:

To the best of my knowledge and belief the above information is absolutely true in every respect.

SIGNED: DATED:

SEND FORM TO: Gyles Brandreth, the Carling Black Label Amazing Almanac, Pelham Books, 44 Bedford Square, London WC1B 3DU.